ST. LOUIS SPORTS FOR KIDS

FOREVER LORE IN THE 314

JOEY ZANABONI

REEDY PRESS

Reedy Press
PO Box 5131
St. Louis, MO 63139
reedypress.com

Library of Congress Control Number: 2025948163

ISBN: 9781681066202

Design by Richard Roden

Front cover images: Arthur Ashe courtesy of Santi Visalli/Getty Images, Ozzie Smith courtesy of Jerry Wachter/Sports Illustrated via Getty Images, Becky Sauerbrunn courtesy of Craig Mercer/MB Media/Getty Images, Kurt Warner courtesy of Focus on Sport/Getty Images, Jordan Binnington courtesy of Dilip Vishwanat/Getty Images, Jackie Joyner-Kersee courtesy of David Madison/Getty Images, Randy Orton courtesy of Ethan Miller/Getty Images

Back cover images: St. Louis CITY SC team courtesy of St. Louis CITY SC, Napheesa Collier courtesy of John Mac, Chris Pronger courtesy of Dave Sandford via Getty images

All images are courtesy of the author or believed to be in the public domain unless noted otherwise.

Printed in Canada

26 27 28 29 30 5 4 3 2 1

Contents

VIEW OF DOWNTOWN ST. LOUIS
CREDIT: MISSOURI HISTORICAL SOCIETY

Introduction

Growing up in St. Louis, I used to watch my dad watch Blues games from the couch. The way he got into the games—cheering, yelling, riding the wave—was as exciting to me as the players on the ice. When I was about 5 he took me to my first game when the barn was called the Kiel Center. It felt like being let into a spaceship and a church at the same time. I'd gone to Clark Avenue in downtown St. Louis and been lifted to a higher, and colder, plane.

When I was 6, my selfless mother was nine months pregnant with twins. Still, she hosted a birthday party in the upper deck of Busch Stadium for me and some friends. We watched a Cardinals game in the late-summer St. Louis heat. Mark McGwire went deep that day. He delivered a home run to centerfield. Mom went into labor the day after and delivered identical twin girls.

The joy of times like those, experienced in my hometown of St. Louis, is pure. I have been blessed with family and friends old and new. These memories and the people who have made them are precious to me. They are something I think about every day, and which I have built my life and my sports announcing career around.

In St. Louis, sports bind us, move us, and reinforce the values that we hold dear: grace under pressure like Kurt Warner; courage to do what's right like Curt Flood. The moments and heroes of the past shine through, even when they're hard to remember. Like sun through slanted blinds, they give us enough light to see our present and chart our future.

Where would we be without track stars to philanthropists like Jackie Joyner-Kersee, tennis pioneers turned public health icons like Arthur Ashe, or underdogs turned inspirational mentors like the 1950 US Soccer team? They are more than heroes. They are friends, role models, and community builders who have gone beyond their games.

Where would sports be without St. Louis? Or, to ask it another way: Where would the world be without St. Louis sports?

The memories you make in this city never go away, no matter how far you go from home. Sometimes those memories are as loud as a playoff crowd, and sometimes they're as soft as the grass on a spring fairway. But they're always there.

Sifting through these stories, legends, myths, and memories to create this book has overwhelmed me with gratitude. I am thankful to have grown up in a city like this.

My one regret is that I could not share more. Among these stories and tidbits, factoids and legends, portraits and photos, are countless others. St. Louis sports history runs like the Mississippi: the risk of flooding is far greater than the risk of drought.

But of course, it's St. Louis, so you know I'm going to write about the high schools. And Nelly.

If my year of work on this book has earned me one thing, then I will take this time to make my wish. Please read something. Anything, honestly. If it's not this book (though you've already read the introduction, so come on!), read something. Please.

Reading real books—books written from a place of truth and compassion—is a promise to ourselves. It is an investment in what kind of future we will have. As Ray Bradbury once wrote, "Without libraries what have we? We have no past and no future." This is a celebration of our past and our future, who we are and who we are to be.

Thank you, St. Louis. These are our stories. This is us.

Joey Zanaboni

MATTHEW AND BRADY TKACHUK
CREDIT: TKACHUCK FAMILY/CHAMINADE

BECKY SAUERBRUNN

CREDIT: NOAH SALZMAN/WIKIMEDIA COMMONS

Acknowledgments

Thank you to all the people who made this book possible. Thank you to Josh Stevens of Reedy Press for coming up with the idea. Thank you to Barbara Northcott for shepherding me through the writing and editing process. Thank you to Dave Lange for acting as a friend and mentor and getting me involved with Reedy Press by inviting me to write the foreword for his own book, *Year One*.

To the players, teams, and individuals who have made their names known in St. Louis sports, every interviewee I sat down with, every person who has dedicated their life to documenting our city's sports history, every person who told me a story about growing up in this city—thank you from the bottom of my heart.

And a special thank-you to the people who have captured our sporting moments through their lenses. I owe a major debt to Justin Barr, Carrie Ogle, Sunshine Lemanak, KMOX Sports, Bill Greenblatt, and the St. Louis Sports Hall of Fame for providing the best pictures. Additionally, certain photographers provided photos via Creative Commons 2.0 Licensing. That license is available here: creativecommons.org/licenses/by/2.0/deed.en.

St. Louis will always be home to me. Thank you to everyone for making it feel that way.

JAMES "COOL PAPA" BELL STATUE AT BUSCH STADIUM

Who We Were and Who We Are to Be

There is simply us,
pouring out in crowds.

I have been with us all my life,
rising as one from our seats

and squinting in the St. Louis sun

at an outfielder stumbling,
flushing blood from our faces.

How quick it turns
and he's off to the races,

Crashing into the padding
and outfield signs,

In his mitt, the ball and game,
how quick they change.

The feelings, the range

Ash crumbling,
risen passion,

"How the heck did he
catch that?"

Funny how a final out
hits us inside

A leaping grab so fine
beauty born from toys

It's game ending
and sending

Midwestern freight trains
of joy

Up and down
our spines.

BASEBALL

St. Louis is a baseball town. Dating back to the mid-1800s, the city's joy and, often, its pride, has been found in the batter's box and on the pitcher's mound. From Cool Papa Bell, Dizzy Dean, and Satchel Paige to Stan Musial, the Wizard, and Albert Pujols, many of the game's greatest players have called our city home.

BIRTH OF A BIRD

The St. Louis Cardinals are founded in 1882. Bat-and-ball pioneer Chris von der Ahe purchases the "Brown Stockings," as the team is originally called. The franchise eventually becomes the "Browns" and then the "Perfectos" in a National League that also features quirky names like the Brooklyn Superbas and the Boston Beaneaters. While the 1899 Perfectos aren't perfecto, they are pretty good, going 84–67. The team becomes the Cardinals the next year.

BEFORE THERE WERE GLOVES

Baseball in the 1860s is a much different game than the modern version. No one wears gloves, and sliding isn't allowed. The ball is thrown underhand. Players regularly rock sweet handlebar mustaches. Today, various St. Louis–based clubs like the Saint Louis Brown Stockings and the Lafayette Square Cyclones offer amateur players the opportunity to play the game under the original rules. Vintage baseball games are played frequently on the Arch grounds.

SLIM PICKINS

Pitchers like Slim Sallee star for the Cardinals in the 1910s. Sallee has an ERA of 2.56 over his career. He wins a "fixed" World Series with the Reds versus the "Black Sox" in 1919. On the field for the Cardinals, the 1910s are generally a struggle. The team does not come within 10 games of the pennant during the decade, but they become heroes in another way.

A BRANCH GREW BEFORE BROOKLYN

Branch Rickey is known best as the executive who helped break baseball's color barrier by signing Jackie Robinson to the Dodgers in the 1940s. But did you know he was both a St. Louis Brown and Cardinal? Hired away from the Browns in 1916, Rickey serves as a Cardinals manager and executive from 1917 to 1942. He designs the minor league system that becomes the standard for MLB teams.

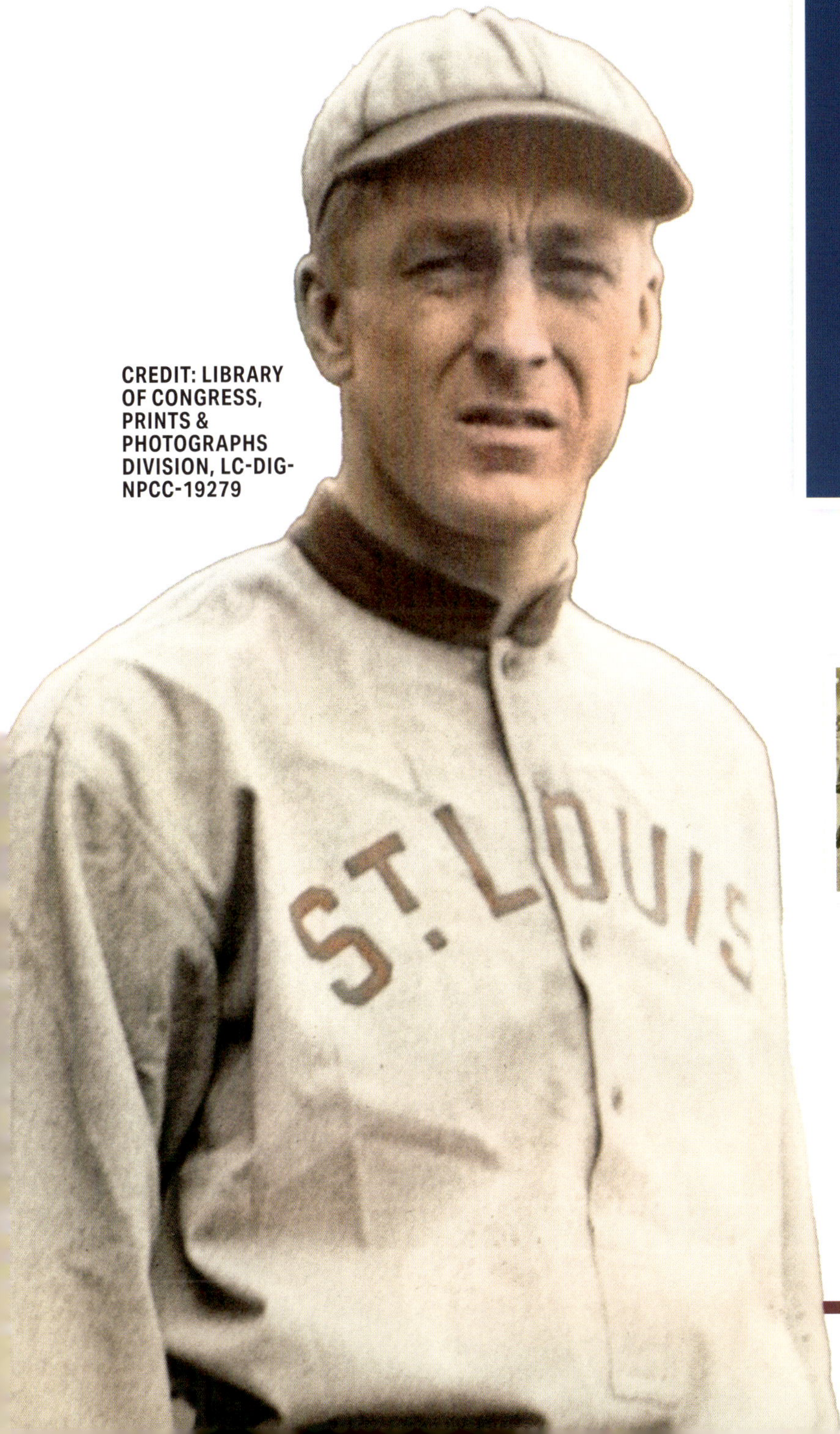

CREDIT: LIBRARY OF CONGRESS, PRINTS & PHOTOGRAPHS DIVISION, LC-DIG-NPCC-19279

Train Wreck

The 1910s are a metaphorical train wreck on the field for the Cardinals. But off the field? Also a train wreck. The 1911 team is best remembered as the group that rescued stranded passengers from a train accident in Bridgeport, Connecticut. The Cardinals' Pullman cars are the only ones that do not fall off the tracks during a serious safety incident. Players, coaches, and staff leap to the rescue, saving many lives. The 1911 Cardinals are not a great baseball team, but they are heroes.

QUEEN HELENE

Did you know the first woman to own a Major League Baseball franchise did it in St. Louis? Helene Britton inherits the Cardinals in 1911 after her father, Frank, and uncle Stanley pass away. Female team owners like Georgia Frontiere and Carolyn Kindle later follow in her footsteps. Britton sells the team in 1917, paving the way for the Branch Rickey era of the St. Louis Cardinals.

THE FEDS

What has St. Louis baseball fans barking like guard dogs at the arboretum in 1914? The St. Louis Terriers and the new Federal League! A new team and league intrude onto the professional baseball season in the early days of World War I, bringing another pro baseball option to St. Louis. Pictured is Harry Chapman, who also plays for the St. Louis Browns in 1916, a year after the Federal League folds.

JUST GORGEOUS

Gorgeous George Sisler breaks hitting records with the Browns in the 1920s to take his place among the all-time greats. One of the most talented batters to ever step in a box, Sisler wins two American League batting average titles plus the MVP award in 1922. His 257 hits in 1920 stand as a Major League record for 84 years before being topped by Ichiro Suzuki in 2004.

GIANTS AND STARS

The St. Louis Stars are born in 1922. Originally the St. Louis Giants, the renamed franchise plays in the Negro National League from 1922 to 1931. Playing home games at Stars Park on Compton and Laclede, the talented group raises three pennants in 1928, 1930, and 1931.

COOL PAPA

The success of the Stars is in large part thanks to James "Cool Papa" Bell. Cool Papa was born in Starkville, Mississippi, before moving to St. Louis as a teenager. The fastest man to ever play professional baseball, he leads the Negro Leagues in stolen bases seven times. His .325 career batting average over a 20-year career lands him in the Baseball Hall of Fame in 1974. Today, his statue stands outside Busch Stadium.

TOP OF THE WORLD

The Cardinals are World Series champs for the first of 11 times! The exciting seven-game 1926 Series versus the New York Yankees climaxes with two outs in Game 7. On the game's final play, catcher Bob O'Farrell makes a heroic throw to Rogers Hornsby to catch a base runner stealing. The out seals the title. That base runner? Babe Ruth.

TIME
The Weekly Newsmagazine

WE'RE GETTING DIZZY

Born in Lucas, Arkansas, the brash Jay Hanna "Dizzy" Dean becomes the leader of the Gashouse Gang. Dean wins 150 games and makes four All-Star teams on the mound. Yet fans always wonder what could have been. Injuries—beginning with a broken toe suffered in the 1937 Midsummer Classic—derail his career, though he later returns to the game as a beloved broadcaster.

GASHOUSE GANG

Future stars Yogi Berra, Joe Garagiola, and other local kids play at Tower Grove and Sublette Parks, imitating Cardinal stars of the decade. Cardinals Dizzy Dean, Ripper Collins, and Ducky Medwick give fans their money's worth in the 1930s. The "Gashouse Gang" notches two more World Series titles in 1931 and 1934.

ONLY HE MAY SPIT

In modern baseball, you can spit on the ground, spit in a cup, and even (accidentally) spit on your friends. But one thing you can't spit on is the ball. A Cardinal is the last to be legally allowed to do that in the 1930s. Burleigh Grimes, a 1931 World Series hero and spitball artist, is "grandfathered in" to new rules after the spitter is banned in 1920. Grimes uses the special "di-spit-sation" to throw the controversial pitch until 1934.

FORTUNE IN THE '40s

There's never been a greater Cardinals team than in 1942. Their 106 wins are still a franchise record. Featuring a roster trained in the original "Cardinal Way," the Redbirds win the World Series in five games against the mighty New York Yankees to usher in the most successful decade in club history.

KHOURY LEAGUE

In 1934, St. Louisan George Khoury hatches a plan to give youngsters a chance to play organized baseball. With the motto "The Khoury League is interested in the child that nobody else wants," he launches what has become the longest-running youth baseball league in the US. The Khoury League is also the first to sort players by age level, putting them into divisions like Midget and Bantam. The league's first game is played in Forest Park in 1936.

SKIP SOUTHWORTH

Best remembered for his successful stint as Cards manager from 1940 to 1945, Billy Southworth did not receive due credit for his contributions until well after his death in 1969. Inducted into the Baseball Hall of Fame in the late 2000s and the Cardinals Hall of Fame in the 2010s, Southworth is one of the most successful managers of the 20th century. He wins World Series titles in 1942 and 1944.

The Man

The Man arrives in St. Louis in 1941. Stan "The Man" Musial debuts for the Cardinals, starting a career that will end with 24 All-Star appearances, three MVP awards, and three World Series. Of his career 3,630 hits, exactly 1,815 came at home and exactly 1,815 come on the road. He is inducted into the Baseball Hall of Fame on the first ballot in 1969 and is awarded the Presidential Medal of Freedom in 2011. Good harmonica player, too.

CREDIT: TRANSCENDENTAL GRAPHICS/GETTY IMAGES

The Streetcar Series

In 1944, the Cardinals and Browns meet to determine the champion of baseball. The Cardinals win the World Series four games to two. The Series is quick. Teams in those days would spend countless days and nights on long train trips. No need in this one—fans and players take streetcars to Sportsman's Park, and the entire six-game set takes less than a week.

PETE'S SAKE

Pete Gray's inspiring story is one of the lesser known in the history of the major leagues. Gray lost his right arm in a tragic mishap involving a wagon as a child. He plays minor league baseball in the early 1940s before signing with the Browns in 1945. That season, the one-armed outfielder compiles 51 hits in 77 games. After a lone year in the majors, he continues to play pro ball through the 1940s and inspires future players like Jim Abbott.

RED OF THE REDBIRDS

Red Schoendienst debuts in 1945 and begins one of the most incredible runs in the history of baseball. He remains in the major leagues as a player, manager, and coach for 74 straight years. A native of Germantown, Illinois, just a half hour's drive from St. Louis, Schoendienst makes 10 All-Star teams and wins two World Series as a player and three as a coach/manager. He serves as skipper of the Cardinals in three different decades.

Mad Dash

The Cardinals win their third World Series of the decade in 1946. Enos Slaughter's "Mad Dash" remains one of the most memorable moments in Series history. He sprints from first on a single—mistakenly scored a double—by Harry Walker with two outs in the eighth inning of Game 7 to score the winning run. It is arguably the boldest baserunning play in the history of postseason baseball. A lifelong Cardinal, Slaughter provides insight, expertise, and knowledge as a coach and consultant in the organization long after his playing days are over.

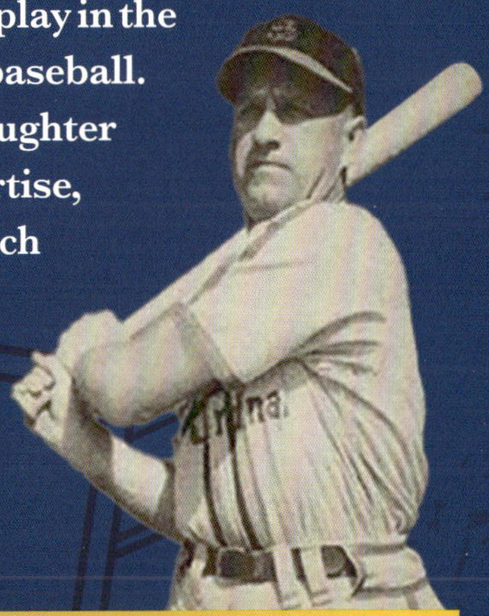

CREDIT: ALL-AMERICAN GIRLS PROFESSIONAL BASEBALL LEAGUE

Girl (Hits for) Power

The All-American Girls Professional Baseball League is originally established in 1943. The goal is to provide another baseball entertainment option with many men serving in World War II. The league endures after the war ends. St. Louisans like pitcher/outfielder Erma "Bergie" Bergman and shortstop Rita Meyer get their chance to play in the AAGPBL during the 1940s and 1950s.

WEAVER/BELIEVER

Earl Weaver graduates from Beaumont High in 1948. The St. Louis–born baseball icon later manages over 2,500 games in Major League Baseball with the Baltimore Orioles, winning the World Series with the team in 1970. Thirty-six years later, another Weaver makes his mark on St. Louis baseball history. Jeff Weaver, a journeyman pitcher acquired midseason, wins the decisive fifth game of the 2006 Series for the Cardinals over the Detroit Tigers.

HOW OLD WOULD YOU BE IF YOU DIDN'T KNOW HOW OLD YOU WERE?

Long held out of Major League Baseball because of segregation, Satchel Paige debuts for the Cleveland Indians at the age of 42 in 1948. He joins the St. Louis Browns in 1951. The ageless wonder earns All-Star selections in 1952 and 1953 during his age 46 and 47 seasons. He stars for Bill Veeck's St. Louis Browns franchise before the team departs St. Louis for Baltimore.

CREDIT: MARK RUCKER/TRANSCENDENTAL GRAPHICS VIA GETTY IMAGES

Veeck, as in Wreck

Bill Veeck had an idea that was short and cleat. Did you know that the shortest player in MLB history played in St. Louis? At three feet, seven inches, Eddie Gaedel enters a Browns game as a pinch hitter in 1951. Wearing the number "1/8," he walks on four pitches. Owner Bill Veeck is the man behind the plan. He is known for his showmanship and his commitment to racial integration, and his autobiography, *Veeck, as in Wreck*, remains a classic.

GUSSIE & BUSCH

Gussie Busch purchases the Cardinals in 1953. Just as he turns the Anheuser-Busch Brewery into the biggest in the world, he turns the Cardinals back into a dominant force. He buys Sportsman's Park outright and eventually builds Busch Stadium II, which opens in 1966. Gussie Busch oversees six pennants and three World Series championships before passing away in the late 1980s.

I'm Just Ken

Ken Boyer is named NL MVP in 1964. A lifelong Missourian, Boyer drives in 119 runs in an era when third basemen are not expected to produce RBI. His jersey is retired by the organization in the mid-1980s. Ken's brother Clete is a third baseman with the Yankees, and the brothers play against each other in the 1964 Fall Classic.

SLATS

St. Louis is blessed by two shortstops in the 1940s who both go by the nickname "Slats." Rita Meyer is born in Florissant and makes a name for herself as a shortstop with the Peoria Redwings of the AAGPBL. Marty Marion, the Cardinals and Browns shortstop, is the 1944 NL MVP and an eight-time All-Star. Billy Southworth dubs him "the best shortstop ever."

THE DEVINE DECADE

Bing Devine is the greatest Cardinals executive to never be in a position of power when the team wins the World Series. In June 1964, Devine is the general manager and makes one of the greatest trades in baseball history (Ernie Broglio for Lou Brock). He is fired two months later when the team sits nine games out in the pennant race. The Cardinals find inspiration down the stretch, win the pennant, and beat the favored Yankees in seven games to win the World Series.

EL BIRDOS

First baseman Orlando Cepeda becomes the team's latest National League MVP with 111 RBI in 1967. The Cardinals win a seven-game World Series over the Boston Red Sox that season. The insane talent on the roster includes Bob Gibson, Curt Flood, Julian Javier, Dal Maxvill, Lou Brock, Steve Carlton, Mike Shannon, Tim McCarver, and Roger Maris. The squad is nicknamed "El Birdos" by Joe Schultz, their first base coach, and is managed by Red Schoendienst. The general manager? Stan Musial.

'68

Devine is rehired as Cardinals general manager going into the 1968 season, when the Cardinals lose a seven-game World Series to the Tigers. The next year the Amazin' Mets win the Series. Their architect? Also Devine, who went to New York after his first St. Louis exit. He later serves as president of the St. Louis Football Cardinals and owns the St. Louis Steamers soccer club in the 1980s.

GIBBY

1968 is "the Year of the Pitcher." The greatest pitcher in the history of the St. Louis Cardinals, Bob Gibson exceeds even his own standard of excellence with a 1.12 ERA, winning both the NL MVP and the Cy Young Award. Whether playing basketball at Creighton and with the Harlem Globetrotters or dominating on the mound, he was the ultimate competitor.

FLOOD'S WARNING

After the 1969 season, center fielder Curt Flood takes a courageous stand against baseball's prejudicial "reserve clause." The reserve clause gives teams ownership of player contracts forever. The player cannot go to another team unless traded. After being traded to Philadelphia, Flood challenges the age-old practice and asks for the ability to choose his next team. Despite facing angry criticism, Flood takes his case to the Supreme Court. The ruling there favors the owners, but the reserve clause is struck down in 1975, allowing players to become free agents.

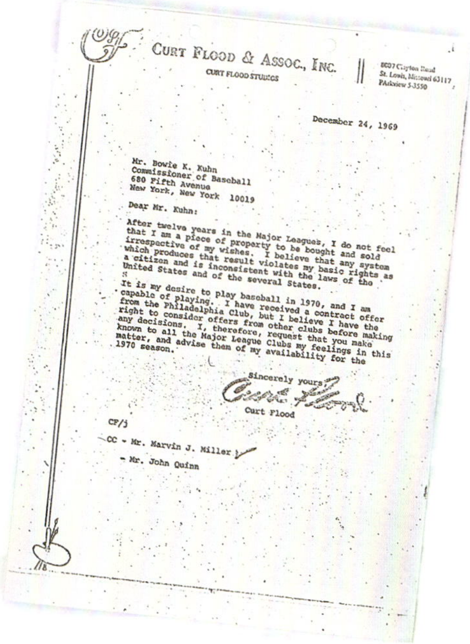

CURT FLOOD & ASSOC., INC.
CURT FLOOD STUDIOS

8007 Clayton Road
St. Louis, Missouri 63117
PArkview 5-3550

December 24, 1969

Mr. Bowie K. Kuhn
Commissioner of Baseball
680 Fifth Avenue
New York, New York 10019

Dear Mr. Kuhn:

After twelve years in the Major Leagues, I do not feel that I am a piece of property to be bought and sold irrespective of my wishes. I believe that any system which produces that result violates my basic rights as a citizen and is inconsistent with the laws of the United States and of the several States.

It is my desire to play baseball in 1970, and I am capable of playing. I have received a contract offer from the Philadelphia Club, but I believe I have the right to consider offers from other clubs before making any decisions. I, therefore, request that you make known to all the Major League Clubs my feelings in this matter, and advise them of my availability for the 1970 season.

Sincerely yours,

Curt Flood

CF/j

CC - Mr. Marvin J. Miller
- Mr. John Quinn

Sweet Lou

A six-time All-Star, Lou Brock sets the single-season stolen bases record in 1974 with 118. Brock breaks Ty Cobb's all-time stolen bases record in 1977. He finishes his career in 1979 with 938 stolen bases. He is the owner of more than 3,000 hits and two World Series rings.

WE NEED SPEED, A WHITE RAT, AND A LOT OF BATS

Led by the White Rat, manager Whitey Herzog, the Cardinals enjoy a renaissance in the 1980s. The team wins three pennants and scores a World Series victory in 1982. The speedy, talented roster includes the Wizard Ozzie Smith, Willie McGee, Vince Coleman, John Tudor, Jack Clark, and Bruce Sutter.

CREDIT: BILL GREENBLATT/ST. LOUIS SPORTS HALL OF FAME

OZZIE

The greatest defensive shortstop ever, Ozzie Smith dazzles fans for the entire decade with his acrobatic play and incredible glovework. He is a 15-time All-Star, a 13-time Gold Glove Winner, and the 1987 Silver Slugger at shortstop. Born in Mobile, Alabama, and a childhood resident of LA, he debuts with the Padres before playing with the Cardinals from 1982 to 1996. He remains active in the organization in retirement.

15-TIME ALL-STAR
13-TIME GOLD GLOVE WINNER

Down to the (McG)Wire

It is the season that "saves baseball." Sinking in popularity after a players' strike in 1994, MLB needs a summer for the ages. It gets one in 1998. Cardinal first baseman Mark McGwire and Cubs right fielder Sammy Sosa battle for the all-time homer crown. They are chasing former Cardinal Roger Maris's hallowed record of 61 home runs. McGwire becomes the first to reset the milestone and finishes with 70 to win the race.

CREDIT: JON GUDORF PHOTOGRAPHY VIA WIKIMEDIA COMMONS

JACK IN THE BOX

"Go crazy, folks! Go crazy!" Jack Buck exclaims on KMOX radio as Ozzie hits an NLCS-winning home run against the Dodgers in 1985. The "home run by the Wizard" propels the Cardinals to the World Series. The euphoric feeling for St. Louisans makes Buck's call the most memorable in the city's history. A World War II vet and part of the Cardinals since 1954, Buck calls games almost right up until he passes in 2002.

Back on Top

In 2006, the Cardinals win the World Series over the favored Detroit Tigers. David Eckstein takes home World Series MVP. Adam Wainwright emerges as a hero after he freezes Carlos Beltran with the bases loaded on a big curve to finish Game 7 of the NLCS. The five-game World Series victory makes Tony LaRussa the first manager to win a World Series in both the American and the National Leagues.

CREDIT: KMOX SPORTS

EL HOMBRE

Albert Pujols debuts in 2011. He astounds St. Louis fans for more than a decade before departing for the Angels. Pujols triumphantly returns to St. Louis to eclipse the 700 home run mark in 2022. Among his numerous achievements in a Cardinal uniform are six Silver Sluggers, three MVPs, three pennants, and two World Series crowns. He is one of only four players in MLB history to hit 700 home runs.

CREDIT: JUSTIN BARR

A New Birds' Nest

Busch Stadium III opens in downtown St. Louis in 2006, and the Cardinals continue a tradition of winning in a new stadium by becoming World Champions. The team began playing in Sportsman's Park in 1920 and won two World Series and three pennants in the following 11 years. The team also won two flags and a World Series to finish the 1960s after moving into Busch Stadium II.

ST. LOUIS'S FAVORITE PHILLIE

The greatest start for any power hitter in MLB history belongs to a batter born in Florissant who graduated from Lafayette High. Ryan Howard hit both 100 and 200 home runs in the fewest games in MLB history. An alum of Missouri State, Howard is named National League Rookie of the Year in 2005 and NL MVP in 2006 plus wins a World Series championship in 2008.

CREDIT: WEASEL BASEBALL LEAGUE

WEASEL FIELD

In the early 2000s, a group of St. Louis youngsters bring an old tradition back in style. Playing at Weasel Field in Christy Park, the local kids play the purest form of baseball: sandlot style. The informal games are known for their fun. The field hosts an annual tournament honoring the life and legacy of Mick McMahon, a Weasel Field player who passed away in a car accident at age 16.

Freese Frame

The Cards are again champions in 2011. A St. Louis native and another Lafayette alum, third baseman David Freese becomes a hometown hero and a World Series icon when he hits a game-tying triple in the ninth and launches a game-winning home run in the 11th to beat the Texas Rangers in Game 6 of the World Series. Pictured: Freese giving the Joplin community hope following a devastating tornado in southwestern Missouri that same year.

CREDIT: STEVE BROOK

INDYBALL

In addition to major-league teams, St. Louis has played host to independent professional baseball. The River City Rascals are three-time Frontier League champions from 1999 to 2019 while playing in O'Fallon, Missouri. The Gateway Grizzlies have called Sauget, Illinois, home since 2001, winning a Frontier League championship in 2003.

YOU CAN CATCH A CHRIS, YOU CAN CATCH A CARP

The bulldog of the Cardinals World Series staff, Chris Carpenter's intensity and drive carry him through a mid-career shoulder injury to a Cy Young Award in 2005 and World Series titles in 2006 and 2011. Carpenter wins Game 5 of the NLDS in 2011 against the heavily favored Philadelphia Phillies, outdueling his longtime friend Roy Halladay in a 1–0 complete game masterpiece. He puts the definitive exclamation point on the season by winning Game 7 of the World Series.

CREDIT: ALL-PRO REELS PHOTOGRAPHY VIA WIKIMEDIA COMMONS

YADI!

The greatest defensive catcher in the history of baseball is a 19-year St. Louis Cardinal. Yadier Molina is the youngest of three Molina brothers who all won World Series titles as catchers for MLB teams. He debuts for the Cardinals in 2004. Yadi wins nine Gold Gloves over the course of the next two decades. He is the only catcher in the MLB history to record over 15,000 putouts.

CREDIT: POLO ASCENSIO

Rippin' Tees, Sippin' Teas

The Cardinals play at West Ham Stadium in London, England, bringing the Cards-versus-Cubs rivalry across the pond in 2023. St. Louis is the home team and rallies from a big early deficit in the second contest to salvage a split in the two-game series. Over 110,000 fans flock to the former Olympic venue for the London Series.

BASKETBALL

Hoops in the Lou . . . From Easy Ed Macauley to Napheesa Collier and Jayson Tatum, some of the best basketball players of all time have called St. Louis home. NBA teams like the St. Louis Bombers and St. Louis Hawks, college programs like Saint Louis University and Washington University and high school teams like Vashon, Incarnate Word, and Chaminade have consistently produced outstanding individual talent. St. Louis basketball lets it fly like a long three and soars like a 360 jam. The city's heart beats to the rhythm of a Spalding on hardwood.

HOOPS DEMO

Basketball is first introduced to St. Louis at the 1904 Olympics. It is a demonstration sport, so there are no official medal winners. But the relatively new American sport finds a new foothold in early 1900s St. Louis. Soon, the sport will come off the bench and into the game.

HE WAS EVEN BETTER AT COACHING FOOTBALL

In 1914–15, under head coach George Keogan, Saint Louis University holds its first men's basketball season. Basketball is just one part of the puzzle for Keogan, who coaches multiple collegiate sports. His greatest success comes in football as the head coach of Notre Dame in the 1920s, '30s, and '40s.

Easy Does It

Saint Louis University becomes the NIT champion in 1948, downing the NYU Violets 65–52. The NIT is then considered to be the true national championship. Ed Macauley is named the tournament's MVP after a superb performance. The 1948 NIT represents the lone major national championship claimed by a St. Louis–area collegiate basketball program.

BALL HAWKS

After finishing in last place in 1954, the NBA's Hawks relocate from Milwaukee to St. Louis. The team almost immediately goes from worst to first. The Hawks were basement dwellers in Milwaukee. After relocating to St. Louis, they finish in third in 1955–56 and make the NBA Finals in 1957.

CREDIT: BETTMANN/GETTY IMAGES

BOMBER RUN

The St. Louis Bombers debut as the city's first professional NBA team in 1949. They are coached by Ken Loeffler (pictured). Saint Louis University High and SLU alum Easy Ed Macauley makes his pro debut with the team. Macauley goes on to a fabulous career that features seven NBA All-Star nods. The Bombers fold after one year in the NBA.

EASY AND PETTIT

The Hawks are champions of the NBA in 1957–58. The championship effort is led by two-time NBA MVP Bob Pettit. Ed Macauley, who arrives with the team in a trade for Bill Russell, is also key. The Hawks peak in 1957–58. They finish 49–23 in the regular season. Pettit drops a 50-burger in Game 6 of the Finals to seal the championship.

HOOPS HOME

Municipal Auditorium is the home of SLU basketball, the champion Hawks, and the St. Louis Streak in the second half of the 20th century. It sees the best of St. Louis basketball for decades. It is renamed Kiel Auditorium in 1943 and closes permanently in 1991 prior to demolition.

JACKIE WHITE

Jackie White is the first African American man to referee an NBA game. He quietly goes about making history in 1968, refereeing a game between the Cincinnatti Royals and the Chicago Bulls in Cleveland. Born in Centralia, Illinois, just an hour's drive from St. Louis, White demonstrates his courage and commitment in another important step in the fight for racial equality in American sports.

Jo Jo White

The US Men's National Basketball Team wins gold in Olympic basketball at the Mexico City games in 1968. The star-spangled squad features St. Louisan Jo Jo White. An alum of McKinley High and the University of Kansas, White goes on to seven NBA All-Star selections with the Celtics. He wins championships in Boston in 1974 and 1976. The incredible point guard is the 1976 NBA Finals MVP.

Something's Bruin at the Arena

The NCAA Men's Basketball Championship is held at the Arena downtown in 1973. UCLA's Bill Walton is the best player in the country, and he proves his greatness under the brightest lights. Many consider his 44-point performance that night to be the most impressive individual performance ever. He makes 21 of 22 shots in front of the St. Louis crowd. UCLA, coached by John Wooden, defeats Memphis State 87–66.

SPIRITS ARRIVE

From 1974 to 1976, the Spirits of St. Louis are the city's American Basketball Association team. They are known as much for their antics outside the St. Louis Arena as for their accomplishments in it. Wild characters like power forward Marvin Barnes make for a memorable two seasons. The ABA folds in 1976, and multiple Spirits go on to NBA careers. That group includes rebounding machine Moses Malone, who ends up in the NBA Hall of Fame.

Bob Ferry

A native of St. Louis, Bob Ferry plays at Saint Louis University in the late 1950s before going on to a solid NBA career in the 1960s. His true calling, though, is in the front office. He builds the 1978 NBA champion Washington Bullets, bringing the only world basketball title ever to DC. A former St. Louis Hawk, he wins two NBA Executive of the Year awards during his post-playing career.

CREDIT: VINCE GENNARO

THE STREAK

In 1979, the St. Louis Streak become St. Louis's first professional women's basketball team. Playing in the Women's Professional Basketball League, the team lasts until 1981. The team represents the only professional basketball option in the city after the Hawks and Spirits depart. Pictured is Jane Ellen Cook, a former Louisiana Techster who becomes an extremely successful high school coach at John Burroughs and Villa Duchesne when her playing days are finished.

CREDIT: DREW YOUNG

Braggin' Rights Nights

Anheuser-Busch revitalizes the Braggin' Rights rivalry between Mizzou and the University of Illinois in 1980. The world-famous sponsor moves the matchup to the St. Louis Arena in 1980. This gives stars like St. Louisan Steve Stipanovich a bigger stage. Illinois wins the first contest at the Checkerdome and nine of 10 rivalry games between the two programs that decade. The Braggin' Rights Game has been a staple in downtown St. Louis for five decades.

IRONS MEN

CREDIT: ADRIAN (AJ) TATUM

The 1985 Vashon boys' basketball team wins one of the most exciting state finals in Missouri history. The Wolverines defeat Soldan 52–49 in OT. The title is one of four that coach Floyd Irons wins in the 1980s. The team features Anthony Bonner, who is later drafted by the Sacramento Kings in the first round of the 1986 NBA Draft. Floyd Irons wins 10 state titles overall at Vashon. His son Tony (pictured here) adds seven more in 10 seasons at the school.

CREDIT: INCARNATE WORD ACADEMY

RED KNIGHTS

Incarnate Word has put together the greatest stretch ever seen in America by a girls' basketball program. The Red Knights win 141 games between 2020 and 2025, a record that will not soon be matched. The unparalleled stretch of success has been orchestrated by head coach/athletic director Dan Rolfes. The program wins an eighth straight state championship in 2025.

Smooth Larry Hughes

Local product Larry Hughes becomes the face of Saint Louis University basketball after an electrifying 1997–98 season. He notches north of 20 points a game. Hughes is an alum of Christian Brothers College High School. Billikens head coach Charlie Spoonhour helps him become a top-10 pick in the NBA Draft. Larry Sr. enjoys a 14-year professional career and mentors his son Larry Hughes Jr., who goes on to play at SLU as well.

CREDIT: KEITH ALLISON VIA WIKIMEDIA COMMONS

CREDIT: BILL GREENBLATT/ST. LOUIS SPORTS HALL OF FAME

NANCY FAHEY

Washington University Women's Basketball wins four straight NCAA Division III titles from 1998 to 2001. Led by Nancy Fahey, the unbelievable run includes a then-national record 81 straight wins. Fahey's program adds another national championship in 2010. She then becomes the head coach at the University of Illinois for five seasons. Fahey is a member of the Women's Basketball Hall of Fame.

DARIUS MILES

East St. Louis's Darius Miles becomes the No. 3 pick in the NBA Draft in 2000. He is selected by the Los Angeles Clippers. Miles is the first ever high school player to be selected with one of the first three picks. He plays for four different teams before injuries force him to retire in 2009.

David Lee

David Lee graduates from Chaminade in 2001 and heads to the the University of Florida. From there, he is drafted by the New York Knicks and becomes an NBA All-Star. He wins a championship with Steph Curry and the Golden State Warriors in 2015 and later marries tennis star Caroline Wozniacki.

CREDIT: KEITH ALLISON VIA WIKIMEDIA COMMONS

CREDIT: @CINDIISSTUFF

Arch Madness

St. Louis plays host to the NCAA Men's Final Four at the Edward Jones Dome in 2005. "Arch Madness" sweeps the area, and the University of Illinois Fighting Illini enjoy plenty of local support. Illinois advances to their first-ever national championship game. The North Carolina Tar Heels, led by head coach Roy Williams and star Sean May, defeat the Illini in the final, 75–70.

CREDIT: UNIVERSITY OF ILLINOIS ATHLETICS DEPARTMENT

CREDIT: JUSTIN BARR

CHAIFETZ

Chaifetz Arena opens in 2008 as the new home of Saint Louis University basketball. The 10,000-plus-seat venue is the brainchild of SLU alum Richard Chaifetz. In addition to hosting great hoops, Chaifetz has become a magnet for concerts like Sabrina Carpenter's Short n' Sweet Tour in 2025.

SURGE FORWARD

The St. Louis Surge women's professional basketball team is founded in 2009. The Surge has enjoyed a successful run featuring a pair of national championships in the Women's Blue-Chip Basketball League. The team currently competes in the Global Women's Basketball Association under the direction of owner/chief executive Khalia Collier.

More Arch Madness

St. Louis has hosted the Missouri Valley Conference men's basketball tournament every year since 1992. The tournament features programs like Creighton, Wichita State, Drake, Loyola of Chicago, and Southern Illinois–Carbondale. On the Division III side, Washington University men's basketball adds back-to-back national titles in 2008 and 2009. They continue to field a strong team with a run to the 2025 Final Four.

Lynx to St. Louis

Napheesa Collier wins her second Gatorade Missouri Player of the Year Award at Incarnate Word in 2015. Collier's incredible determination and skill take her to national championship glory at UCONN, back-to-back gold medals at the Olympics, and four WNBA All-Star selections (so far) with the Minnesota Lynx.

CREDIT: JOHN MAC

CREDIT: KEITH ALLISON VIA WIKIMEDIA COMMONS

Big Panda

Bradley Beal wins the 2011 Gatorade National Player of the Year award while leading a powerhouse Chaminade program. Like former Chaminade big man David Lee, Beal plays college ball at Florida. He is the third overall pick in the NBA Draft in 2012. The teenage phenom plays with the Washington Wizards from 2012 to 2023 before joining the Phoenix Suns. Did you know? Teammates call him Big Panda because he can eat ginormous meals.

TATUM PLAYED 'EM

Jayson Tatum leads Chaminade Prep to the Missouri 5A State Championship in 2016. Coached by Frank Bennet, Tatum wins the Missouri Gatorade Player of the Year award in three consecutive seasons before heading to Duke. He is drafted by the Boston Celtics and leads them to an NBA Championship in 2024.

BOWLING

A history of sports in St. Louis that spares bowling? Bud, that's not possible. Get your head out of the gutter and come walk a mile—or at least to the foul line—in our rental shoes. St. Louis enjoys as rich a bowling history as any city in the country. The original home of the International Bowling Hall of Fame and the birthplace of tenpin superstars like Ellen Kelly and Pete Weber, the Lou has lanes that span the sport's history.

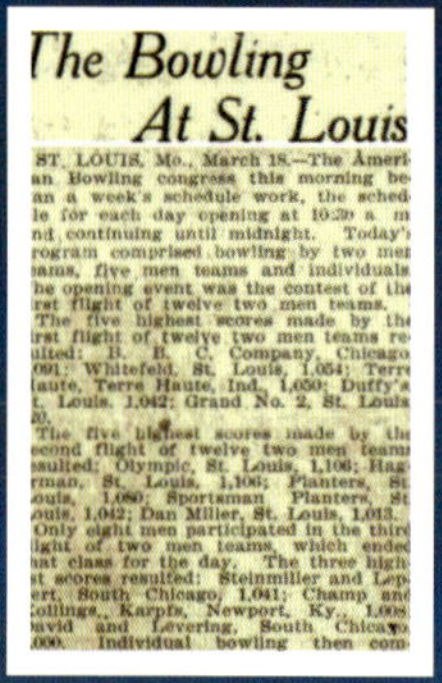

The Bowling
At St. Louis

ST. LOUIS, Mo., March 18.—The Ameri-an Bowling congress this morning be-an a week's schedule work, the sched-le for each day opening at 10:30 a. m nd continuing until midnight. Today's rogram comprised bowling by two men eams, five men teams and individuals he opening event was the contest of the rst flight of twelve two men teams.

The five highest scores made by the rst flight of twelve two men teams re-ulted: B. B. C. Company, Chicago 091; Whitefeld, St. Louis, 1,054; Terre laute, Terre Haute, Ind., 1,050; Duffy's t. Louis, 1,042; Grand No. 2, St. Louis 30.

The five highest scores made by the econd flight of twelve two men teams esulted: Olympic, St. Louis, 1,106; Hag-rman, St. Louis, 1,106; Planters, St ouis, 1,080; Sportsman Planters, St ouis, 1,042; Dan Miller, St. Louis, 1,013.

Only eight men participated in the third light of two men teams, which ended hat class for the day. The three high-st scores resulted: Steinmiller and Lep-ert, South Chicago, 1,041; Champ and Collings, Karpis, Newport, Ky., 1,035 avid and Levering, South Chicago, 000. Individual bowling then com-

THIS ONE'S FOR THE GIRLS

The first all-female bowling league in the country takes root in St. Louis. In 1915 the St. Louis Women's Bowling Association begins, thanks to the efforts of local resident Ellen Kelly, who helps the organization find its feet in the role of secretary. The first version of the Women's National Bowling Association begins the next year in 1916. Kelly's team, appropriately named "Progress," wins the 1916 Women's International Bowling Congress championship.

The 1937 Hermann Undertakers

A score so good you'll think you've been cracked in the head with a bowling pin. . . . The five-man Hermann Undertakers roll a team mark of 3,797 across three games. This is a record in Masters competition that stands for 21 years. According to legend, the feat happens at Floriss Lanes, though reporters of the time say Del-Mar Lanes. Floriss plays host to another incredible, record-breaking bowling night two decades later.

EIGHT LANES UPSTAIRS

Saratoga Lanes famously has "eight lanes upstairs." Maplewood's favorite bowling alley and pool room has stood the test of time, whizzing past its 100th birthday like a perfectly measured strike roll. Walk up and see it sometime. Saratoga is the oldest bowling alley west of the Mississippi River.

The Budweisers

This Bud's for Buds. Five fine individual bowlers transform into the most dominant bowling team ever in the 1950s and 1960s. Sponsored by Anheuser-Busch brewery, the Budweisers are more than just a marketing gimmick to sell beer. The team sets the standard for bowling teams everywhere, competing in tournaments and exhibitions across the country and world.

CREDIT: IBMHOF AND ANHEUSER-BUSCH, INC. PHOTOGRAPHIC DEPARTMENT

WEBER & SON

Dick Weber arrives in Florissant from Indianapolis in 1955. He quickly becomes the key piece of the fabulous Budweisers squad that dominates professional bowling across two decades. His career includes over 30 PBA titles and a spot on the St. Louis Walk of Fame. He is the father of Pete Weber, the high-octane bowling sensation who will later take the sport by storm.

Mr. Bowling

Born in St. Louis in 1926, Don "Mr. Bowling" Carter enjoys one of the most distinguished playing careers in American bowling history. He is widely recognized as the greatest player of his era. Carter is elected as the first president of the Professional Bowlers Association (PBA) in 1958. His national fame leads to a million-dollar endorsement deal with bowling manufacturer Ebonite in 1964. With inflation, that's about $10 million today!

BOWLING ON TV

St. Louisans aren't just good at bowling. We're also good on TV. Behold proof of that in Jack Buck and Nelson Burton Jr. Buck, better known as the voice of the Cardinals, is also a prominent bowling announcer in the early 1960s, calling *Top Star Bowling* on television. Bo Burton has a jaw-dropping, pin-dropping career featuring 18 PBA titles. His national fame really expands, though, as he becomes a broadcaster with ABC in the 1970s.

"WHO DO YOU THINK YOU ARE? I AM!"

Pete Weber, son of Dick, goes pro in 1979 and wins 10 major championships, including five US Opens. In 2012, an ESPN clip of his infamous celebration after winning one of those Opens goes viral. The video features Pete wildly and proudly screaming and snarling the eternal question: "Who do you think you are? I AM!!!" Displaying the passion that makes bowling in St. Louis special, it remains an internet meme.

CREDIT: CARRIE OGLE/PBA

IBMHOF

Like a pin being placed from above, the International Bowling Museum and Hall of Fame is gently positioned near Busch Stadium in Downtown St. Louis in 1993. The hall is massive: 50,000 square feet—or bowling shoes, if you prefer. The IBMHOF shares the building with the Cardinals Hall of Fame and remains a vibrant attraction before relocating to Arlington, Texas, in 2010.

CREDIT: INTERNATIONAL BOWLING MUSEUM & HALL OF FAME

CREDIT: VANDERBILT UNIVERSITY

COLLEGE GAME

St. Louis has been the site of phenomenal professional bowling through the years. It has also been an important city for college bowling. Tropicana hosts the NCAA women's bowling championship in both 2015 and 2018, with Nebraska and Vanderbilt (pictured) becoming champions.

2020s

St. Louis's vibrant bowling scene continues on with renowned establishments like Pin-Up Bowl in the Delmar Loop, Tropicana Lanes in Richmond Heights, and Kingpin Lanes in Florissant going strong. Whether you go for 10 pins, 10 pints, or just as an excuse to wear someone else's velcro shoes for awhile, STL bowls on.

Nelly, Nelly, Nelly

It's gettin hot in herre . . . When you think of Olympic Lanes, there are many memorable moments, records, and family nights. It opens in 1973 as *the* spot before eventually falling on hard times. Enter Nelly. The St. Louis hip-hop mogul announces that he has purchased the lanes in 2025 with big plans for significant renovations. The new lanes will be called Dirty Bowling.

CREDTI: SOPHIA SCHELLER/REVIEWSTL

BOXING

For most of the 20th century, boxing is the most popular and important sport in America. It is king, and St. Louis is a royal throne room. The greatest boxers ever have lived in, trained in, fought in, and passed through the rings of this city. We are known for our grit and our underdog mentality. Virgil Akins, Hurricane Henry Armstrong, and Sonny Liston define a generation's fighting spirit and then pass it on. That fighting spirit continues through the champion brothers Leon and Michael Spinks and modern names like Devon Alexander and Jessica McCaskill. The town that literally gave the world boxing gloves knows how to pull itself off the canvas and pack a punch.

WHY DON'T WE WEAR GLOVES INSTEAD?

What is boxing without gloves? It's how they fought before 1903 (and for a little while after). Credit St. Louis with introducing this important safety measure. In 1903, the city hosts the first world championship bout that requires both fighters to wear gloves. Abe Attel wins the bout against Johnny Reagan.

OLYMPIC RINGS IN THE RING

Boxing is introduced as an Olympic sport during the Summer Games at Forest Park. The men's bracket features 18 fighters, all from the United States. Samuel Berger wins the heavyweight gold. The World's Fair celebration also features an exhibition-only women's division. This is a pioneering step for female boxing, but it is short-lived. Female boxing will not appear as an Olympic sport again until the London Games bring it back in 2012.

The Champ

Future heavyweight champion of the world Sonny Liston moves to St. Louis as a teenager in 1944. Born in Arkansas, the "Big Bear" is incarcerated in the Missouri State Penitentiary for robbery in 1950. He uses the adversity to learn the art of boxing under Rev. Alois Stevens. His local ties come to the forefront in 1953 when he and 10 other St. Louis Golden Gloves champions fight a team of Western European boxers at Kiel Auditorium in 1953.

CREDIT: STANLEY WESTON/GETTY IMAGES

LEGACY OF LISTON

Liston debuts professionally in St. Louis late in 1953. He wins the world heavyweight title in 1962. He has two famous showdowns against Muhammad Ali in the mid-1960s. He loses both bouts. Liston dies tragically young at 38 but serves as a major inspiration for later heavyweight champions like Mike Tyson.

HURRICANE

Hurricane Henry Armstrong wins the featherweight belt in 1937 before claiming titles in the lightweight and welterweight classes. He is the only man ever to hold three divisional championship belts at the same time. Armstrong is a graduate of Vashon High School and a member of the International Boxing Hall of Fame. He continues to be rated as one of the greatest fighters in the history of the sport.

CREDIT: SOUTH BROADWAY ATHLETIC CLUB

VIRGIL

Virgil Akins is born March 10, 1928, in a riverside neighborhood in downtown St. Louis. "Honeybear" wins the world welterweight belt at the age of 30 in 1958 by defeating Vince Martinez. Akins remains in the history books as a St. Louis icon, becoming the first native-born St. Louisan to claim a world championship belt. This mural at South Broadway Athletic Club by Christian Guémy honors his legacy.

McCaskilla

Jessica McCaskill is a former Golden Gloves champion who wins welterweight titles in 2018 and 2019. She is from Belleville and is also a lightweight champion. McCaskill's success has been stunning, especially when you consider that she did not even start boxing as an amateur until she was 24. Her meteoric rise and her resilience are impressive.

12TH AND PARK

CREDIT: CHRISTOPHER RYAN, STL.ORG

St. Louis boxers continue to grow and thrive at facilities like the 12th and Park Recreational Center. The boxing program there is run by Harold "Champ" Petty. Petty is a former five-time Golden Gloves champion who mentors and trains young boxers. Many young fighters train under him as they chase belts like the one he earned in the North American Boxing Federation in 1982 as a bantamweight.

Leon

The brothers Leon and Michael Spinks each win gold medals in Montreal in 1976. The brothers grow up in St. Louis's Pruitt-Igoe projects. They train in boxing as a means of fending off bullies. In 1978, Leon Spinks upsets Muhammad Ali to claim the world heavyweight title. An alum of Vashon, he fights professionally only seven times before taking on Ali in Las Vegas for the belt. Spinks wins the fight in a split decision, becoming the world champion.

JINX

CREDIT: BILL GREENBLATT/ST. LOUIS SPORTS HALL OF FAME

The younger brother of Leon, Michael "Jinx" Spinx wins the world light heavyweight title in 1983. Also an alum of Vashon, Michael goes on to hold the world heavyweight title from 1985 to 1988. Nicknamed "Jinx," Spinks goes 31–1 over his professional career. For Michael "Jinx" Spinks and his older brother Leon, it started in north St. Louis.

Semper Fi

Hoorah! The Marines fight first responders in the First to Fight event in St Louis in 2009. The charity event raises money for organizations like Toys for Tots and Backstoppers. The well-received event is held at the home of the Blues.

GUNS 'N HOSES

A St. Louis tradition, "Guns 'n Hoses" is born in 1987. It is originally called the St. Louis Metro Boxing Showdown. The exhibition event honors first responders, most famously featuring boxing matches between St. Louis police officers and St. Louis firefighters. The event has become a cornerstone of the community, with funds raised being used to help the families of fallen first responders through the Backstoppers charity. Today it has expanded to other sports like soccer as well.

CREDIT: ST. LOUIS BUDWEISER GUNS 'N HOSES

CREDIT: JOE MURPHY/GETTY IMAGES

CORY SPINKS AND DEVON ALEXANDER

Leon Spinks's son Cory reigns as the undisputed welterweight champion of the world from 2003 to 2005. His nickname is "The Next Generation." He holds multiple belts throughout his career. Here Cory poses at Guns 'n Hoses with his uncle Michael Spinks and Devon Alexander, a former Junior Olympics champion from Hyde Park. Alexander wins the light welterweight world title in 2009 and the welterweight belt in 2012. Alexander is nicknamed "The Great."

CHESS

Emanuel Lasker once said, "When you see a good move, look for a better one." Though the insightful world chess champion was born in Prussia and died in New York City, his observation on the sport could describe the royal game's progress through St. Louis. Each time the city has made a good move in chess, it has followed up with a better one. Now home to the World Chess Hall of Fame, St. Louis has its place in history not among the pawns, rooks, knights, or bishops, but among the kings and queens.

Long Time

CREDIT: MISSOURI HISTORICAL SOCIETY

Judge John Fenton Long wears a lot of hats in mid-1800s St. Louis. A police commissioner, a customs collector, a judge, and a city father, Long is also a noted chess player and a friend of General Ulysses S. Grant. Prior to the Civil War, the two are known to engage in long games of chess together using the chess set pictured here. Who knows how these contests affect Grant? Does he learn lessons in strategy for the bloody chess game that follows from 1861 to 1865?

YES TO CHESS

The year is 1886. Ah, the days of the first President Grover Cleveland administration. . . . St. Louis stakes its claim to chess history by hosting, in part, the Chess World Championship. Wilhelm Steinitz triumphs over Johannes Zukertort in the championship match but not in the battle of difficult-to-pronounce names.

BIGGEST YEAR EVER

In 1904, St. Louis hosts the World's Fair, an Olympics, and the Seventh Annual Chess Congress. The Missouri Athletic Club hosts the Congress, and St. Louisan Max Judd demonstrates the city's talent. Judd puts St. Louis on the map (I mean, board). He founds the St. Louis Chess Club and helps transform the city into a king among players.

BET ON WOLBRECHT

George H. Wolbrecht is the victor at the Western Chess Association (WCA) National Championship in 1906. The event is later rebranded as the US Open Chess Championship. Born in Hamburg, Germany, Wolbrecht immigrated to St. Louis and established it as an important piece on the national grid. An alum of Washington University, which looked like this when he attended, he wins the WCA crown once again in 1910.

THE FINEST CHESS CITY IN AMERICA

St. Louis hosts its third US Open Chess Championship in 1941, and Reuben Fine wins the event for the third straight year. The city is now the center of the game for much of the country. St. Louis boasts popular playing spots like the thriving Downtown YMCA Chess Club. Chess is black and white. But, in the 1940s and 1950s, a golden hue has settled over the board in the city.

WHY IS BOBBY FISCHER THE ONLY CHESS PLAYER WE EVER HEAR ABOUT?

Robert H. Steinmeyer is perhaps St. Louis's most important player, dominating the competition beginning in the 1940s. His fascinating match versus Bobby Fischer in 1963 at the US Championships marks a major moment in the careers of both players. Like the legendary Fischer, Steinmeyer inspires a generation of chess fans to make their own moves.

CREDIT: EAST ST. LOUIS HIGH SCHOOL

Flyers Chess

The East St. Louis Flyers Chess team dominates the St. Louis area game in the 1970s and '80s. The program wins three straight St. Louis high school chess championships during the era. It even features future NFL star Kellen Winslow, who turns in a perfect record in 1975. The Flyers are remembered for their state final run of 1978 and for being one of the most formidable programs ever in the Metropolitan Inter Scholastic Chess League.

CREDIT: THE SAINT LOUIS CHESS CLUB

The Founder

Jim Davies founds the Missouri Chess Association in 1973. He has an impactful playing career and increases the reach of chess during his days at Missouri State and throughout his life in St. Louis. Davies is the first-ever Missouri Chess Hall of Fame inductee. He earns the induction in 2000.

KING REX MAKES A MOVE

The St. Louis Chess Club opens in July 2008 in the Central West End. The brainchild of St. Louis businessman Rex Sinquefield, the club's tournament hall becomes a hot spot for the best players in the region and country. The club hosts tournaments like the Sinquefield Cup and the Monday Night Mania Blitz as well as grand prix events like the Blizzard Bowl.

STANDING IN THE HALL OF FAME

The World Chess Hall of Fame relocates to St. Louis in 2011, combining with the St. Louis Chess Club to form a campus at the center of the chess universe. The hall of fame's guiding principle reads: "The mission of the World Chess Hall of Fame is to educate visitors, fans, players, and scholars by collecting, preserving, exhibiting, and interpreting the game of chess and its continuing cultural and artistic significance."

ABOVE AND TOP RIGHT CREDIT: WORLD CHESS HALL OF FAME & GALLERIES/ST. LOUIS CHESS CLUB

A DECADE OF DOMINANCE

Grandmaster Susan Polgar and Webster University establish a chess team, leading to national championships every year from 2013 to 2017. The incredible run inspires an arms race across collegiate chess that is concentrated in the St. Louis area. The Saint Louis University Billikens emerge as a powerhouse as well, winning the 2022 President's Cup, the national championship of collegiate chess.

CREDIT: WEBSTER UNIVERSITY

Gorlocks, Billikens, and Tigers

In 2023, under coach Liem Le, Webster captures a sixth national title, equaling the most in college chess history. The President's Cup national championship is held in St. Louis, and the final stage of four teams features not only Webster but also the Saint Louis University Billikens and Mizzou Tigers. Checkmate, everywhere else. St. Louis is the king of the American game.

CORKBALL

How far from—and how close to—home a tiny ball flies. At the turn of the century, St. Louis invents a sport that takes over its streets and alleys and soon spreads across the country. First played at a saloon on Grand during the horse-and-buggy days, corkball endures through vibrant local clubs today. In St. Louis, as in corkball, there really is no base but home.

Born in a Saloon

Relaxing after an American League game earlier that day, the St. Louis Browns take a break at Mueller's, a saloon on Grand. The team's owner, Chris von der Ahe, is the manager of Mueller's. So he doesn't mind when the players take a cork out of a barrel. They use the cork and a mop handle to play the first-ever game of corkball. The Browns invent a new sport and then finish 20 games over .500 in their other one. The squad's 78–58 record is good for third among 16 Major League teams.

BASEBALL WITHOUT BASES

Finally, it's baseball without the inconvenience of running the bases! All you need is a pitcher, a catcher, and a batter. The growing game now features a long, thin bat and a tiny horsehide ball. The game varies based on the area in which it is played, which can include cages. In tight quarters, all hits are singles. With more space, lines are drawn 100 feet from the plate for a single, 150 feet for a double, 200 feet for a triple, and 250 feet for a home run. Players bat; ghosts run. There is no base but home.

DOUGHBOYS OF SUMMER

While preparing for action in World War I, St. Louis boys use sticks to play corkball in Arkansas fields around their training ground. The doughboys, as American soldiers are called at the time, love a game that travels easily. The Soldiers Memorial Military Museum downtown honors the memories of the 156,000 St. Louisans who fought in World War I.

IT'LL CORK

Corkball booms in the 1920s into the 1930s. The RH Brady Company manufactures the first official corkball, and the Rawlings plant follows suit. Markwort Sporting Goods begins manufacturing corkball equipment and becomes an important and famous supplier.

BLUE MONSTER

CREDIT: TONY MINOR

The Gateway Corkball Club is founded in 1929. The club still exists today. It has a membership that spans all age groups. Its headquarters and field are on Walsh Street. The club codifies rules and organizes league play in the 1920s and '30s. Their facility features the famous Blue Monster, a massive wall in left field of "corkball heaven." Gateway is the oldest corkball club in the world.

CREDIT: TOM ORGAN

WHEN WE WERE YOUNG

The Grupp Corkball League becomes the second officially established club in the city in 1936. The club is known for being home side of Don Young, aka "Mr. Corkball." In addition to his expert playing, Young helps establish the first citywide corkball tournament in 1979. Today, the corkball fields at Jefferson Barracks Park are named after him.

USS *BUNKER HILL*

The USS *Bunker Hill* is deployed in the Pacific during World War II. Sailors take their minds off the war by playing corkball. To keep the ball from flying into the sea, they design cages aboard the ship's deck to play in. The cage idea quickly makes its way to dry land. Local St. Louis establishments follow suit. Bars, restaurants, and clubhouses add cages to the sides of their buildings as corkball enters its golden age.

Lemay Corkball Club

CREDIT: LEMAY CORKBALL CLUB

The Lemay Corkball Club is born in 1947. One of the oldest corkball clubs in the city, Lemay Corkball Club continues to be a pioneer in advanced corkball stats in the modern day. Lemay Corkball Club keeps detailed statistics on the club website and stat tracking apps. This proves that corkball is set for success in the 21st century.

UNCORKING MY OWN STORY

The author of this book discovers a corkball, bat, and catcher's half mask in the toy chest of his grandparents' home around 1995. He proceeds to hit seven home runs, three triples, a double, and another home run. A year later, he sees his first actual, real-life pitch from his older brother and forgets to swing.

CREDIT: SPORTSMAN'S CORKBALL CLUB

SPORTSMAN'S

Sportsman's Corkball Club is established in 1957. Sportsman's plays at Tower Grove Park and later moves to Jefferson Barracks. They are the last of the four major St. Louis clubs. The club takes great pride in it motto, "The Most Prestigious Corkball Club in the World." It cohosts the citywide tournament each year.

CREDIT: TOM ORGAN

World Series

The first ever citywide corkball tournament is held in 1979. The championship event continues to attract a healthy crowd into the 2020s. Played at Jefferson Barracks Park, the series combines all of the corkball clubs with great food and fun vibes. Competition runs high, and, in the town that invented the sport, the winner is truly the world champion.

FOOTBALL

St. Louis football: hard-hitting, fast, and tough. Like a fullback blocking downfield, St. Louis football has paved the way for the rest of the country. The city invents the forward pass at the beginning of the last century and wins the Super Bowl at the end of it. From Bradbury Robinson to Marshall Faulk, St. Louis's history is packed with examples of coaches, players, and fans who have refused to be defined by limits. In this city, there are no end zones. Only touchdowns.

SMASHMOUTH ALL-STARS

The St. Louis All-Stars debut in 1923. The city's original professional football team, the All-Stars are owned by Ollie Kraehe, who also coaches the team and plays on its offensive line. The All-Stars share Sportsman's Park with baseball's St. Louis Browns. The All-Stars win one of seven games in their inaugural season. The win is notable. It comes against the Oorang Indians, whose roster includes Jim Thorpe (pictured), by a final of 14–7. The team's money problems force it to fold at the end of the 1923 season.

Billikens Fresh off a Bender

The Blue and White become the Billikens in the 1910s because of their coach. John Reinhold Bender, a collegiate coach across multiple sports, is said to resemble the Billiken. The mythical Billiken is a Japanese charm popular in America in the early 1900s. The Billiken nickname sticks for the entire football team and eventually becomes the Saint Louis University (and Saint Louis University High) mascot.

CONZELMAN'S GUNNERS

The St. Louis Gunners are added to the NFL during the 1934 campaign. The team is based at the St. Louis Armory and is sponsored by the Missouri National Guard's 128th Field Artillery Unit. In 1935, the Gunners join the American Football League and, later, the Midwest Football League. Jimmy Conzelman of St. Louis is the team's original head coach.

Chile Walsh

A University of Notre Dame alum, Chile Walsh becomes the premier St. Louis football coach of the 1930s. Walsh coaches Saint Louis University from 1930 to 1933 before joining the Gunners. Interestingly, he wins the Super Bowl in 1945 with the Rams as the team's general manager. They are neither the St. Louis nor the Los Angeles Rams at the time, though. The Rams of the early 1940s play in Cleveland.

Serve with Honor

Harvey J. Jablonsky is named an All-American at Washington University in 1929. Jablonsky represents the best of St. Louis sports. Like many other great athletes from St. Louis, he attends a service academy and dedicates his life to the cause of preserving freedom. After Washington University, he goes on to another All-American selection on the West Point offensive line. He has a long, distinguished career in the US military.

STOP RUNNING OR HISTORY WILL PASS YOU BY

The first forward pass in football history is thrown in 1906. The program? Saint Louis University. Bradbury Robinson finds Jack Schneider. The play is designed by head coach Eddie Cochems, who watches from the sideline as the pass is completed against Carroll College in Waukesha, Wisconsin.

Pitchin' Paul

Pitchin' Paul Christman, quarterback of the Chicago Cardinals, wins the NFL Championship against the Philadelphia Eagles in 1947. Christman is a former player at Maplewood–Richmond Heights High. He is also a Mizzou Tiger, enjoying an immensely successful college career under the guidance of the legendary Don Faurot. When his playing days are done, he becomes a prominent football announcer and analyst.

Coach WEEB EWBANK, Baltimore Colts

WORLDWIDE WEEB

Weeb Ewbank coaches the Washington University Bears football team to big success in the late 1940s. He records a 9–1 record in 1948 before going on to win NFL championships with Johnny Unitas and the Baltimore Colts in the 1950s. As head coach of the Jets in 1965, he wins Super Bowl III and makes good on his quarterback Joe Namath's much-publicized guarantee to beat Unitas and the Colts.

POP IVY

Former Oklahoma All-American Pop Ivy serves as the original head coach of the St. Louis Cardinals football team in 1960–61. The Sooners alum is a successful Canadian Football League coach before assuming the head coaching duties of the Chicago Cardinals in 1958. He remains with the team, relocating to St. Louis for the 1960 season.

Big Red

The St. Louis Cardinals join the NFL in 1960. The Big Red plays at the original Busch Stadium and Busch Stadium II until 1987, after which they become the Phoenix (and eventually Arizona) Cardinals. They are the longest-tenured NFL team to call St. Louis home. The team never wins a Super Bowl but does win the NFC East Division twice in the mid-1970s and makes three playoff appearances.

CREDIT: MISSOURI HISTORICAL SOCIETY

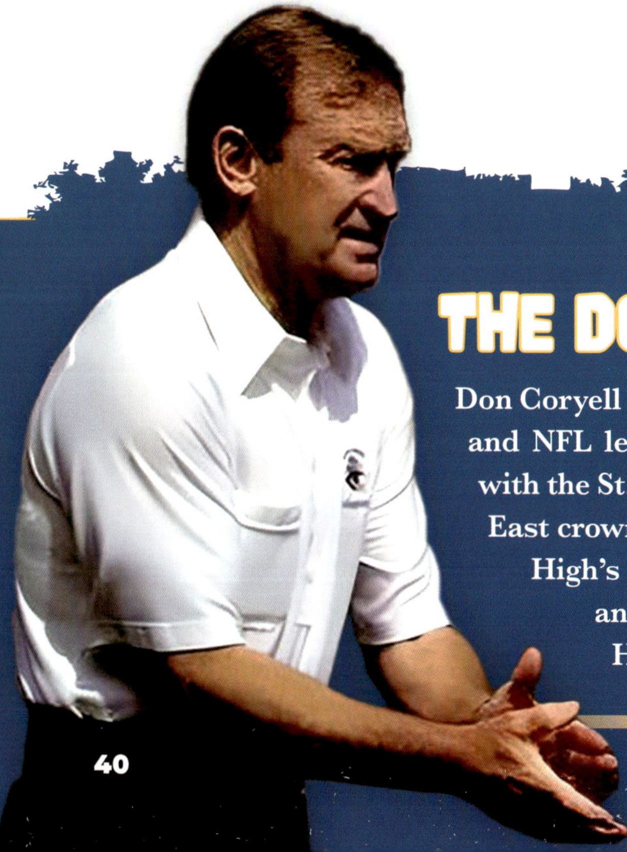

THE DON

Don Coryell is the only man to win 100 games at both the college and NFL levels. He makes the leap from college to the pros with the St. Louis Cardinals in 1973. The team then earns NFC East crowns in 1974 and 1975. He later coaches East St. Louis High's Kellen Winslow with the Chargers. Both Coryell and Winslow have earned induction into the Chargers Hall of Fame.

BIRDS OF A FEATHER

Famous Cardinals of the 1960s and 1970s include four-time All-Pro quarterback and SIU Carbondale alum Jim Hart; five-time All-Pro safety Larry Wilson; four-time Pro Bowler Mel Gray, whose 1975 "Phantom Catch" versus Washington springboarded the Big Red to a division title; and offensive tackle/broadcaster Dan Dierdorf. The most beloved yet hated, though, is Conrad Dobler, whom *Sports Illustrated* called "the NFL's dirtiest player" in 1977.

ROGER KNOWS ROGER

A high school prodigy in King City, Missouri, and a former star at Mizzou, cornerback Roger Wehrli earns five All-Pro selections from 1970 to 1977. He enters Canton as a Hall of Famer in 2007. Famed Dallas Cowboys quarterback Roger Staubach pays him the ultimate compliment, saying famously that "the term 'shutdown corner' originated with Roger Wehrli."

WIN FAST, WINSLOW

1974–75 is a huge year for receivers in St. Louis. Mel Gray makes the Phantom Catch, and Kellen Winslow graduates from East St. Louis High School, ringing up an all-conference honor in his only year as a high school football player. Winslow is also an undefeated member of East's chess team. He goes on to an All-American career at Mizzou and is a member of the NFL's All-Decade Team for the 1980s while starring with the Chargers.

Medium Green Machine

Roy Green is an '80s revelation for the St. Louis Cardinals. The six-foot wide receiver earns back-to-back All-Pro honors in 1983 and 1984, leading the league in touchdowns in 1983 and receiving yards in 1984. The Henderson State alum stars in all three phases of the game across his career, also playing safety and returning kicks. He spends 12 of his 14 years in the NFL with the Cardinals.

Greatest High School Football Coach Ever?

The East St. Louis Flyers win three straight state titles from 1983 to 1985 and are named one of the six best-ever high school football teams by ESPN. Their incredible run includes a 44-game winning streak. Their GOAT coach is Bob Shannon. The head coach of East St. Louis for 20 seasons, Shannon wins two national championships and six state titles, and his teams make the state championship game eight times.

DIVINE TURNAROUND

Pope John Paul II holds Mass at TWA Dome on January 27, 1999, as part of a two-day trip to the United States. The Mass, which features a packed house at the home of the Rams, may be a sign of a divine turnaround for the local football team. The Rams had never finished over .500 in any of their first four seasons in St. Louis. All of that changes, though, in 1999.

STEVE ATWATER

LEAD A HORSE TO WATER, LEAD A BRONCO TO ATWATER

Steve Atwater is drafted by the Broncos in 1989. A Lutheran North alum and an Arkansas Razorback, Atwater goes on to eight Pro Bowl selections as a hard-hitting safety. He wins back-to-back Super Bowls with Denver in the 1997 and 1998 seasons. He gains Hall of Fame status and a gold jacket in 2020.

SAINT LOUIS RAMS

Multiple attempts to bring an NFL franchise back to St. Louis culminate in 1995. The Los Angeles Rams relocate to St. Louis and are greeted with immediate enthusiasm as they begin play at the TWA Dome downtown. St. Louis fans make every game in the franchise's first 12 seasons a sellout.

RIGHT TIME

CREDIT: J.D. SMITH

After going 4–12 in 1998, the St. Louis Rams are widely regarded as an NFL also-ran entering the 1999 season. But the team has quietly improved under head coach Dick Vermeil. When Vianney alum Trent Green suffers a knee injury during the preseason, an unknown quarterback named Kurt Warner assumes the reins of the offense. He throws 41 touchdown passes to the likes of Marshall Faulk, Isaac Bruce, and Torry Holt, going 13–3 and leading the franchise to its first Super Bowl appearance since the move to St. Louis.

The Night It Truly Became the Georgia Dome: A New Frontiere

CREDIT: CARLOS ANTONIO LEON

There is a long tradition of strong female ownership in St. Louis sports. Georgia Frontiere is the owner of the Rams in the Super Bowl season. Born in St. Louis and an alum of Soldan, the former *Today* show host relocates the Rams to her hometown of St. Louis in the 1990s. When the team wins the Super Bowl, the game takes place, appropriately, at the Georgia Dome in Atlanta.

GREATEST SHOW ON TURF

The Rams become the first Super Bowl champion of the new millennium on January 30, 2000. A 73-yard touchdown pass from Warner to Bruce with two minutes left breaks the 16–16 tie against the Tennessee Titans. A game-saving tackle by linebacker Mike Jones on the one-yard line as time expires seals the 23–16 victory. As of 2024, Vermeil, Warner, Faulk, Bruce, and offensive tackle Orlando Pace have been inducted into the NFL Hall of Fame.

CREDIT: JEFF HAYNES/AFP VIA GETTY IMAGES

Vermeil

Coach Dick Vermeil has one of the most unusual paths to a Super Bowl championship in NFL history. The head coach of the Eagles in the 1980s, he reaches but loses a Super Bowl before retiring for 15 years. Surprisingly, he comes out of retirement to coach the Rams in 1997. He wins the Super Bowl in 2000 and retires after the game, handing off the coaching duties to Mike Martz. Vermeil later comes out of retirement again to coach the Kansas City Chiefs.

BRUUUCE AND HOLT

The dynamic wide receiver pairing who lead the Rams to Super Bowl glory, Isaac Bruce and Torry Holt set the standard for wideouts in St. Louis. Bruce, a four-time Pro-Bowler and Hall of Famer, catches the first and last passes of the team's playoff run. Holt, a rookie during the magical season, reels in a Super Bowl TD too. Torry Holt (pictured here) goes on to post more receiving yards than any other player in the NFL in the 2000s. It's a travesty that he is not in the NFL Hall of Fame as of this writing.

2001—A CHASE ODYSSEY

Marshall Faulk wins the NFL's Offensive Player of the Year Award as the Rams win another Western Conference crown in 2001. He totals 2,147 yards from scrimmage as the Rams score an astounding 503 points over a 14–2 season. The team suffers heartbreak in the Super Bowl, though, as the Patriots, led by a young Tom Brady, win on a last-second field goal 20–17.

CREDIT: TOM HAUCK VIA GETTY IMAGES

The Tackle

Mike Jones rises to the occasion on the do-or-die last play of the Super Bowl. Targeted by Titans QB Steve McNair and wide receiver Kevin Dyson, Jones adjusts back after Dyson catches a short slant. He makes "the Tackle" at the one-yard line. He later goes on to coach locally at Saint Louis University High, where his program produces NFL talent like New York Jets safety Tony Adams.

AMERICAN UNDERDOG

He's the greatest underdog story, the greatest Cinderella-only-he's-a-football-playing-fella story in American sports history. Kurt Warner comes out of nowhere. The 28-year-old former Arena League quarterback is left available for the expansion draft before the season. When every other team passes on signing him, he earns the starting job plus regular season and Super Bowl Most Valuable player awards. An NFL Hall of Famer, Warner continues to be involved in humanitarian projects in the St. Louis community.

CREDIT: FOCUS ON SPORT/GETTY IMAGES

ART OF MARTZ

Described as the most impactful coaching pickup in NFL history by Dick Vermeil, offensive coordinator Mike Martz immediately turns around the Rams' struggling offense in 1999. It is his preparation of Warner as the team's backup that pays the biggest dividend. Martz serves as the Rams head coach from 2000 to 2005 and is an alum of Washington University in St. Louis.

CREDIT: SPORTING NEWS VIA GETTY IMAGES

CREDIT: ST LOUIS SLAM WOMEN'S FOOTBALL

CREDIT: THE FAMILY ARENA

The Slam

The St. Louis Slam debut in 2003. The Slam are members of the National Women's Football Association and have remained active over the last 20 years. The team is one of the most successful in league history, winning 124 of 162 games from 2003 to 2024 and most recently hoisting the Women's Football Alliance championship trophy in 2024. The Slam have called the campus of St. Mary's High School, now known as South Side Catholic High School, home since their inception.

RENEGADES WHO HAD IT MADE AND THEN RAGED

The St. Louis Renegades, an indoor professional football team, begin play at the Family Arena in 2001. The team later rebrands as the RiverCity Renegades, the Show-Me Believers, and the RiverCity Rage from 2001 to 2009. The franchise relocates to Iowa years later. Though short lived, the team paves the way for indoor football teams like the Battlehawks.

CREDIT: KENTON MILLER

KEEP THE TEAM!

In 2016, the Rams relocate to Los Angeles, where they had previously been based from 1946 to 1994. I don't want to talk about this one. It still hurts. I'll just lean on the fans, who wear jerseys that say "Stay in STL" and chant "Keep the team! Keep the team! Keep the team!" at the 2015 regular season finale.

FOOTBALL IS FOR EVERYONE

Michael Sam is the Southeastern Conference Co-Defensive Player of the Year at Mizzou in 2013 after tying the school record with 11.5 sacks. He enters the 2013–14 NFL Draft with more than just an impressive résumé of defensive excellence. Drafting him means drafting the first openly gay player in the history of the NFL. While other teams pass, the Rams select him in the seventh round. Sam accepts the Courage Award at the 2014 ESPYS, an award named after another pioneering St. Louisan: Arthur Ashe.

TURKEY DAY

It's a Thanksgiving tradition unlike any other as Kirkwood and Webster Groves battle it out for the coveted Frisco Bell trophy. This rivalry game dates back to 1907. Kirkwood High alum Jeremy Maclin stars at Kirkwood and Mizzou before becoming a 2014 Pro Bowl selection with the Philadelphia Eagles. He becomes head coach of the Pioneers program in 2021.

10K

The greatest running back in St. Louis history? Most fans say Marshall Faulk, but Steven Jackson also makes a strong case. Jackson is an alum of Oregon State and a two-time All-Pro while playing for the Rams from 2004 to 2012. He is the only Los Angeles or St. Louis Ram to rush for over 10,000 yards while playing for the team.

CREDIT: DILIP VISHWANAT/GETTY IMAGES

CREDIT: CARRIE OGLE

KAW IS THE LAW

KaKaw! The St. Louis Battlehawks debut as part of the the XFL. Playing in front of packed crowds at the Dome at America's Center, the Battlehawks make national headlines for fan support as they lead the league in attendance. The team continues to participate in the United Football League and has featured such players as former Alabama quarterback AJ McCarron (pictured).

STALLIONS IN ST. LOUIS

St. Louis hosts the UFL Championship game between the Birmingham Stallions and the San Antonio Brahmas. The Brahmas defeat the Battlehawks 25–15 in the conference championship round but are annihilated 25–0 by Birmingham in the final. UFL CEO Russ Brandon praises the football culture and community of St. Louis when choosing the championship site. The game is played in St. Louis again in 2025.

Mizzou to the Lou

College football comes to St. Louis in a big way in 2023. Tiger Nation shows out at the biggest collegiate football event of the decade in St. Louis. The Mizzou to the Lou game against Memphis is a massive success at the Dome. Under head coach Eli Drinkwitz, St. Louisans Brady Cook and Luther Burden III lead Mizzou to an exciting 34–27 victory.

CREDIT: SCOTT KANE/GETTY IMAGES

GOLF

Ah, golf . . . the chirp of the birds, the clink of the putter, the gentle breeze blowing the blades of grass on a majestic fairway. The peacefulness of a warm spring afternoon. The angry throwing of the club after slicing on 11 . . . sheesh, now I'm talking about my last round. What happened to the peacefulness?

St. Louis golf has been the tee box for pioneers of the game and out-of-this-world characters who won Major championships. St. Louis's golf history runs longer than a perfectly struck John Daly driver straight down the fairway. From Chandler Egan to Tiger Woods, the greatest players ever have played in one of America's most historic and welcoming golf cities.

Chandler's Chance

Chandler Egan stars at the Summer Olympics in 1904. The collegiate champion the same year at Harvard, Egan captures the Olympic team gold at Glen Echo Country Club in Normandy and adds a silver in the individual category. Afterward, the Olympics drop golf from their schedule for more than a hundred years. The next golfers to hang medals around their necks won't do it until 2016.

LISTERINE DOESN'T TASTE AS SWEET AS VICTORY

Albert Bond Lambert also medals at the 1904 Summer Games as part of another American team. He earns the silver in the team event. A native of St. Louis, he hails from a wealthy and important family in the city. His father, Jordan W. Lambert, is the coinventor of Listerine mouthwash. Albert is also an ace aviator. His friendship with Charles Lindbergh inspires the name of the plane that Lindbergh flies across the Atlantic: the *Spirit of St. Louis*.

FOPOGOCO

Golf in Forest Park extends back as far as the late 1800s. In 1912–1913, the park adds 18 holes officially. Forest Park is the first public course in the St. Louis area. The course is situated in the largest park contained within city limits in America. It becomes a refuge for golfers of all backgrounds, including African American players. The local Black players of the time overcome racial discrimination on the way to more equal access to the course.

Keeping Up with the Jones

The US Amateur Championship is held on the western side of the Mississippi for the first time in 1921. That year, the US Amateur comes to Clayton. St. Louis Country Club hosts the tournament. Jesse Guilford wins the event, which also features a young Bobby Jones. The prestigious championship returns to St. Louis in 1960.

THE DISTRICT

CREDIT: SLDGA

Representatives from clubs across the area form the St. Louis District Golf Association in 1916. The SLDGA enacts a formal agreement to encourage cross-club competition. It initially includes Bellerive, Glen Echo, and Algonquin. Today, there are 25 members. St. Louis golfer extraordinaire Bob Cochran is an outstanding early player. He wins a junior district championship in 1931 and a senior district championship 40 years later plus state championships at all levels in between.

RANKIN' WITH THE BEST OF THEM

Judy Rankin wins the Missouri Amateur in 1959. The 14-year-old's victory launches an incredible career. Her victory list includes 26 LPGA Tour victories and back-to-back years at the top of the LPGA money list. She has earned other honors, including a *Sports Illustrated* cover and the LPGA Lifetime Achievement Award in Journalism.

PLAYERS' PLAYER

The US Open comes to Bellerive Country Club in Town and Country in 1965. This is the first time St. Louis has hosted the tournament. Golf superstars like Jack Nicklaus, Arnold Palmer, and Gary Player vie for the title. Player wins the event to complete a career Grand Slam.

ALWAYS CHECK YOUR SCORECARDS, KIDS

CREDIT: AUGUSTA NATIONAL/GETTY IMAGES

In 1968, Bob Goalby becomes the first St. Louisan to win the Masters, golf's biggest tournament. Goalby's title comes in strange fashion. His coleader, Roberto De Vicenzo, submits an inaccurate scorecard following the final hole, resulting in a one-stroke penalty. The Belleville native Goalby is declared the champion.

CREDIT: BILL GREENBLATT/ST. LOUIS SPORTS HALL OF FAME

HAAS TO BE JAY

St. Louisan Jay Haas wins the NCAA Individual Men's Championship in 1975 at Wake Forest. His Demon Deacons team is one of the greatest ever in college golf. Haas wins nine times on the PGA Tour and finishes in the top three at the 1995 Masters and the 1999 PGA Championship. Haas is the nephew of Bob Goalby. He and St. Louis golfer/broadcast icon Peter Jacobsen are inducted into the St. Louis Sports Hall of Fame (pictured) in 2020.

CREDIT: JIM LEEKER

JAY BIRDIE

An alum of Saint Louis University High, Jay Delsing has been instrumental in growing golf in the city. He is the son of former St. Louis Brown Jim Delsing. A UCLA alum, Jay cards over 500 events on the PGA Tour. He has been a driving force behind the Ascension Charity Classic at Norwood Hills and the Gateway FootGolf Classic at WingHaven Country Club in O'Fallon.

ALL HALE

CREDIT: UNIVERSITY OF COLORADO GOLF

Hale Irwin has his name on the US Open trophy three times over. He plays collegiately at Colorado (pictured here) before going on to make history at the pro level. A native of Joplin, Irwin is a longtime resident of St. Louis. Hale Irwin is one of only two players to win the US Open three times. He accomplishes the feat in 1974, 1979, and 1990. The only other player to win it three times? Tiger Woods.

They Won't Leave Bellerive

CREDIT: BELLERIVE COUNTRY CLUB

St. Louis golf fans lift Bellerive Country Club to new heights at the PGA Championship. Over 200,000 fans come out for the four-day championship event. Brooks Koepka shoots a record –24 to win the major. Tiger Woods, who finishes second, praises the local crowd, saying, "The people here were so positive, the energy was incredible, but the positiveness of it all. . . . There were no negative comments, no one was jeering, no one was making snide remarks, everyone was just very positive."

Long John

Long John Daly is known for his two Major championships and more than two wild escapades. Did you know that Daly is a former Missouri state high school golf champion? While he was not born in St. Louis, his love of the Cardinals and his entertaining play at the Ascension Charity Golf Classic will forever connect him to the city. He once even threw a ceremonial first pitch off the backstop at Busch Stadium.

CREDIT: DILIP VISHWANAT/GETTY IMAGES

HOCKEY

Compared to Madison, Wisconsin, or St. Paul, Minnesota, St. Louis is not necessarily the coldest city. But when it comes to hockey, we'll go up against any city, any temperature, any time. From the early days of the St. Louis Flyers and the St. Louis Eagles to the Stanley Cup season in 2019 for the Blues, hockey history is very important in this city. Now our cherished hockey tradition is flying through the cold arena air like an Al MacInnis slapshot bound for the back of the next century's net.

Turn of the Century

CREDIT: UNSPLASH

The St. Louis Ice Palace opens at Grand Center in 1899. The first indoor ice rink in St. Louis, it is similar to the Winter Garden, a cold attraction constructed for the World's Fair. The Ice Palace hosts hockey, figure skating, speed skating, and recreational events before it is demolished in 1963.

THE ST. LOUIS FLYERS

The St. Louis Flyers become the first professional hockey team to call St. Louis home in 1928. Formerly the Winnipeg Maroons, the team is a member of the American Hockey Association and, later, of the American Hockey League. The Flyers bring six regular-season championships and five postseason championships to the St. Louis Arena before folding in 1953.

SENATORS LOVE EAGLES

The city gets its first taste of NHL hockey with the St. Louis Eagles. Running out of money, the Ottawa Senators make a risky move. They relocate to St. Louis and play one season as the Eagles in the mid-1930s. The team struggles on the ice, finishing last in the Canadian Division despite being located a long way from Canada. The club disappears at the end of the 1935 season.

Penalty Shot!

The Eagles make history in November of their one season. In downtown St. Louis against Montreal, Ralph "Scotty" Bowman benefits from a new rule. He becomes the first-ever NHL skater to score on a penalty shot. Funny enough, another Canadian guy named Scotty Bowman becomes more well-known in St. Louis hockey lore. Thirty years later, that Scotty Bowman takes over as head coach of the St. Louis Blues.

BETTER BUY A ZAMBONI

In 1967, the NHL expands with six new teams, including the St. Louis Blues. Under the ownership of Sid Salomon Jr., Robert Wolfson, and Stan Musial, the Blues open play at the Checkerdome. "St. Louis Blues" is a popular ragtime song by W.C. Handy. It provides the basis for the team's new name.

BIRTH OF THE BLUES

The St. Louis Blues emerge as the Western division's most powerful team in the late 1960s. They make a run to the Stanley Cup Final three straight years and win division titles in 1969 and 1970. Red Berenson leads the team in scoring the first year. The Blues are one of the most successful expansion teams ever in American sports. Yet, in three years, the team goes 0–12 in Stanley Cup Final games versus Montreal and Boston.

Plante Yourself in Front of the Goal

One of the 100 Greatest Players in NHL history, Jacques Plante plays for six NHL teams from 1947 to 1975. After a brief retirement, just shy of his 40th birthday, he becomes the Blues goalie in 1968–69 and into the 1970 playoffs. In his final game with the team, he suffers a head injury on a slap shot that breaks his mask. He recovers and continues his incredible career in Toronto.

JR

Who is the first player the Blues ever drafted? The Blues select Montreal Canadiens defenseman Jim Roberts in 1967. He spends four-plus seasons with the team before returning to Montreal. The Toronto native is honored with special "JR" insignia on the Blues helmets when he dies in 2015. He enters the team's Hall of Fame 10 years later.

My Teammates Are like Brothers . . . Actually They Are My Brothers

Three brothers define the early Blues. Bill, Bob, and Barclay Plager all played with the Note on their chest from 1968 to 1972. The tough-minded but fun-loving trio are called the "Battling Brothers." Of the three, Bob plays the longest with the Blues (11 years). He later serves as coach of the team. Today, the Plager rinks at the Centene Community Ice Center are named after the first family of St. Louis hockey.

BARCLAY PLAGER

CREDIT: STEVE BABINEAU/NHLI VIA GETTY IMAGES

WHAT'S LIFE WITHOUT CHALLENGE?

CREDIT: DE SMET JESUIT ATHLETICS DEPARTMENT

Missouri high school hockey holds its first state Challenge Cup championship in 1972. The St. Louis Blues and Union Electric combine forces to sponsor the inaugural event. It is held at the Arena and features eight St. Louis schools. The De Smet Spartans become the first ever Challenge Cup champs. The Blues provide the championship trophy.

Burnin' Bernie

A St. Louis Blue from 1976 to 1989, "Burnin'" Bernie Federko is an all-time Blue. He is also a popular commentator for the team. He plays the most games in franchise history (927) and holds the records for most career points with the team (1,073) and assists with the team (721). His frank and often hilarious analysis of the Blues' play has endeared him to St. Louisans of all ages.

SUSTAINED SUCCESS

The Blues of the 1980s establish a winning tradition rarely seen in professional sports. Beginning in the 1979–1980 season, the team rattles off 25 straight years making the playoffs. Brian Sutter, Brett Hull, Paul Cavallini, Rob Ramage, and Mike Liut, among others, emerge as the team's new crop of stars in the 1980s.

A SAD TRUMPET IN A SASKATCHEWAN BLIZZARD

The biggest threat to the Blues streak of bringing playoff hockey to downtown St. Louis? A nearly successful attempt to relocate the team to Saskatoon. The NHL's board of governors, citing a number of concerns, blocks the move in 1983. Somewhere in the cold Canadian night, wind whipping snow wildly, a sad trumpet plays the Saskatchewan Blues. . . .

Great (Thirty) One

The Great One is a Blue, at least for a little while. Wayne Gretzky averages more than a point per contest in 31 games, including the playoffs, after being traded to the Blues in 1996. He also feuds with often-angry head coach Mike Keenan. Gretzky departs St. Louis after the season to finish his career with the New York Rangers. Still, he and his wife, Janet, who hails from St. Louis, have a house in Frontenac. He has frequently cited his love for the city.

THE GOLDEN BRETT

Brett Hull holds the record for most goals scored in a Blues sweater. He finds the back of the net 527 times while playing in St. Louis from 1988 to 1998. The Hall of Famer is the son of fellow Hall of Famer Bobby Hull, aka "The Golden Jet." Playing with Adam Oates and Scott Stevens, Brett scores 86 goals in 1990–91 in one of the greatest seasons in NHL history.

CREDIT: FOCUS ON SPORT/GETTY IMAGES

Y2K

CREDIT: DAVE SANDFORD VIA GETTY IMAGES

The Blues win the franchise's first Presidents' Trophy in 2000. The Presidents' Trophy is given to the team that earns the most points in the regular season. Head coach Joel Quenneville builds the league's best defense with goalie Roman Turek, captain Chris Pronger, and lightning-shooting Al MacInnis. Pavol Demitra and Pierre Turgeon lead the team's offense as the Blues accumulate a franchise-record 114 points.

JUNIOR BLUES

The St. Louis Junior Blues are a junior hockey organization that finds national success in the mid-2000s, winning four straight Junior B national championships. The organization currently competes in the North American Hockey League Tier III, or NA3HL. The Jr. Notes play most of their home games at Affton Ice Rink across from Grant's Farm.

CREDIT: ST. LOUIS JR. BLUES

SNAKES ON SKATES

The St. Louis Vipers play downtown at the Kiel Center in the 1990s as part of Roller Hockey International. Bernie Federko coaches the inaugural team. In 1999, the Vipers win the Murphy Cup before folding. The franchise is resurrected at the Family Arena in St. Charles in 2019 to compete in the National Roller Hockey League. The team never plays, though. The COVID pandemic disrupts the plans of the team and league.

WICKENHEISER

Doug Wickenheiser scores the glorious "Monday Night Miracle" overtime goal in the conference final versus Montreal on May 12, 1986. The Blues win three division titles with Wickenheiser's help in the 1980s. Wickenheiser is diagnosed with cancer in the mid-1990s, and his battle against the disease inspires many. To this day, no other Blue has worn No. 14. Missouri state high school teams compete for the Wickenheiser Cup, a trophy named in his honor.

You Otter Know

In 1999, the Missouri River Otters begin play in the minor-league United Hockey League. The Otters skate on ice laid at the Family Arena in St. Charles. The team peaks in notoriety in 2004 when four Blues, including Barret Jackman (pictured), join the roster during the National Hockey League lockout.

CREDIT: ALEX RICH

HOCKEY AT A BASEBALL STADIUM

The NHL Winter Classic comes to Busch Stadium in January of 2017. The rink is built on the storied baseball field. The Blues defeat the Blackhawks by a final of 4–1. The comeback effort sees three goals scored in the third period, all by the home team. As of early 2025, the Blues are a perfect 3–0–0 in Winter Classic events.

LONG WAY UP TO THE CUP

Assuming the GM duties in the early 2010s, Doug Armstrong becomes the architect of the Blues Stanley Cup run. He makes the decision to install Craig Berube as head coach. "Chief" assumes the interim head coaching duties from Mike Yeo in November of 2018. From there, he engineers the most spectacular turnaround in NHL history, taking the Blues from dead last in January to Stanley Cup champs in June.

The Dream Comes True

The dream comes true in the most improbable fashion imaginable. In last place on New Year's Day, the St. Louis Blues make the playoffs as the eighth seed. They then go on a miracle run that ends with a Stanley Cup. The team features captain Alex Pietrangelo, Alexander Steen, Pat Maroon, Vladimir Tarasenko, Ryan O'Reilly, David Perron, Brayden Schenn, and goalie Jordan Binnington. They win four road games against the Bruins, including a thrilling seventh game in Boston, to take the Cup.

BANDITS

In 2006, the St. Louis Bandits form in the North American Hockey League. They call the Summit Center in Chesterfield home from 2006 to 2012. They make the Robertson Cup national final in their last year as a franchise. Alums include future Blue Pat Maroon and former Blue Kelly Chase, who is part owner in the team. The Bandits are often thought of alongside the Heartland Eagles, a United States Hockey League team that plays in Chesterfield in 2003–2004.

CREDIT: TOM CALHOUN

THE MOST CONSISTENT MAN IN THE NHL

There are so many great voices associated with the Blues on the air, from Dan Kelly and Gus Kyle to Ken Wilson to John Kelly and Chris Kerber. How about in the arena? Anyone who has been to a Blues game knows him. Tom Calhoun has served as the Blues PA man since 1987, delighting Blues fans with his steady, memorable voice and unflappable consistency. He is known for his ironman streak of never missing a game. He is also the PA voice of the Gateway Grizzlies.

CREDIT: JUSTIN BARR

WE WENT BLUES!

Half a million St. Louisans flock to Market Street for the Blues' victory parade. The festivities feature former star Brett Hull hilariously leading the crowd in a "We Went Blues!" cheer. The cheer is a play on the popular chant "Let's Go Blues!" at Enterprise Center. The dreams of so many come true with that cup. It is only fitting that the celebration itself becomes exactly that: a wild, wonderful dream.

JON HAMM, JENNA FISCHER, AND THE NHL ALL-STARS

In the afterglow of the Stanley Cup win, St. Louis hosts the NHL All-Star Game in early 2020. Held at the Enterprise Center, the game features the game's brightest stars, as well as St. Louis–born celebs like Jon Hamm and Jenna Fischer. Jeremy Boyer, the team's longtime organist, keeps the party going well above the ice.

TKACHUK PUCK

CREDIT: TKACHUK FAMILY/ CHAMINADE

In the 2020s, Chaminade alums Matthew and Brady Tkachuk become the faces of the NHL. The sons of former Blue Keith Tkachuk, both are NHL All-Stars. Matthew is the captain of the Florida Panthers, who win the Stanley Cup in 2024 and 2025. Brady is currently the captain of the Ottawa Senators. Both are also alums of the AAA Blues program and Chaminade. Pictured: The brothers bring the cup back to their alma mater Chaminade in 2024.

CREDIT: VILLA DUCHESNE

FIELD HOCKEY

Villa Duchesne Field Hockey has won a Missouri state record 15 Midwest Field Hockey Championships. The program wins a nail-biter of a final against the John Burroughs Bombers in 2024. The Saints have won multiple titles in each decade dating back to the 1980s. The Frontenac-based school has won four of five Midwest titles to start the 2020s.

Lions Have Claws; Lions Have Blades

Centene Community Ice Center in Maryland Heights opens in 2019. Best known as the new official practice facility of the Blues, the multirink gem also hosts the Lindenwood Lions. The Lions dominate the American Club Hockey Association before their top ACHA team goes NCAA Division I in 2022. The men's NCAA Division I team scores its first win against Air Force in October of that year.

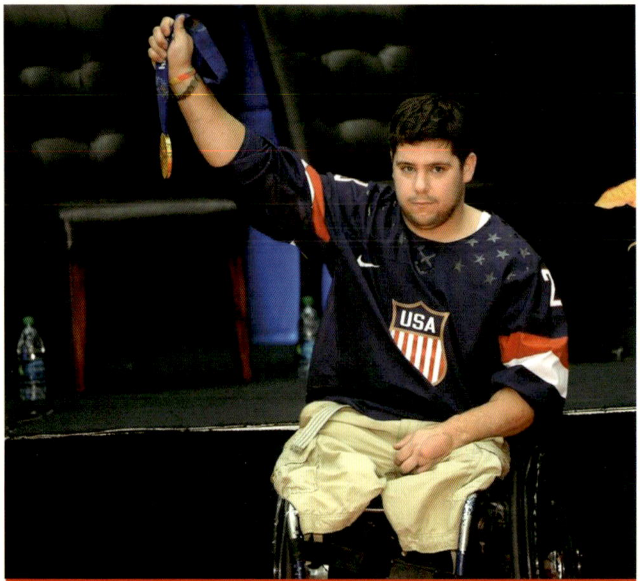

CREDIT: DOD NEWS FEATURES VIA WIKIMEDIA COMMONS

Hockey Is for Everyone

The USA Disabled Hockey Festival comes to St. Louis in the early 2020s. Centene hosts the event in 2023 and has also been the site of USA Sled Hockey games. Sled hockey games at the facility between Team USA Sled Hockey and Team Canada are well attended. The games show that the future of the sport is bright for all players, coaches, and fans in St. Louis.

OLYMPICS

If you're first at the Olympics, you are the best in the world. And we were first. St. Louis holds the important distinction of being the first American city to host the Olympics. Held in Forest Park and other locations around the city, the Olympics came to St. Louis as part of the 1904 World's Fair, also known as the Louisiana Purchase Exposition. From bizarre events to trailblazing competitors, the Olympics in St. Louis will never be forgotten.

GOLD IN THEM WATERS

Charles Daniels stuns the swimming world by winning a gold medal in the gentle waters of Forest Park. At a time where few thought that Americans were any good at swimming competitively, Daniels wins gold in the 220-yard individual freestyle event. He is part of the New York Athletic Club four-man team that wins the 4 × 50 relay as well. The third-place finishers in that event? The Missouri Athletic Club.

Olympic Rings, Olympic Things

St. Louis plays host to the 1904 Summer Olympic Games as part of a greater celebration: the World's Fair. The games last more than four months and feature 95 events, including boxing, which debuts as an Olympic sport. Francis Field on the campus of Washington University is home to track and field events. The aquatic competitions are held at Creve Coeur Lake and Life Saving Lake in Forest Park.

Plungers

The 1904 Games are remembered for their local flair and their somewhat bizarre take on sports. Events include the long-distance plunge, in which competitors battle to see how far they can sink themselves in the lake at Forest Park. The once-popular sport itself goes underwater shortly after the 1904 Games. It will never again be an Olympic event.

TUG OF WAR

Two teams. One rope. Zero reasons we should not make this an Olympic sport again! From 1900 to 1920, you could win a medal by pulling a glorified piece of string harder than the other team. Southwest Turnverein of St. Louis teams take silver and bronze in 1904. Can you imagine Olympic superstars like Michael Phelps and LeBron James in a tug of war gold medal match? Let's make it happen, people.

Fake News, Fake Lose

You can fake anything nowadays: your news, your eyelashes, and your Instagram profile. Can you fake an Olympic sport, though? (And I'm not talking about breakdancing either, Raygun.) Faker Frederick Lorz attempts to fake out the Olympics during the 1904 marathon, riding his way across 26.2 miles in a friend's automobile. It almost works, too. He is briefly considered the winner before the plot is unraveled.

HERO OR CHEAT?

It eventually becomes clear that Thomas Hicks is the real winner, though Hicks himself may not know it. He is repeatedly "dosed" with performance-enhancing drugs by a team of helpers who meet him discreetly along the course. The dehydration and the various substances make him start seeing and imagining crazy things. The hallucinations are so bad that Hicks barely knows where he is as he crosses the finish line to become the first ever American-born marathoner to win an Olympic gold.

History Made

For all their silliness, the Forest Park Olympics do provide a platform for individual greatness. It is a pre–World War era. Society is both deeply flawed and yet somehow more innocent than our own time. For four months in 1904, athletes excel on the world stage to prove that there is no such thing as impossible. It is fitting that the first modern Olympics held in America take place in St. Louis.

SPRINT FOR EQUALITY

At an Olympic Games often stained by racism, George Coleman Poage calmly becomes the first African American to medal at the modern Olympics. His top-three finishes in the 200-meter and 400-meter sprints are well-deserved results in an improbable story. Born in Hannibal, Missouri, Poage travels just over 100 miles from his birthplace to take his place among the best in the world.

THE X MAN

Franz X. Kugler becomes the first and only Olympian to earn a medal in three different sporting categories at the same Games. The German immigrant makes his home in St. Louis and medals in wrestling, tug of war, and weight lifting. His feat in weight lifting later comes under scrutiny: He earns a bronze when only three people competed! Everybody got a medal! His longtime commitment to St. Louis, though, where he dies in the 1950s, is never in question.

Golden Girls, Golden Gloves

The 1904 Olympics offers a women's boxing exhibition/ demonstration event. Though there are no medalists in the event, the ring gives women a chance to show what they can do. This was not always the case and certainly would not be so afterward. The 1904 women's boxing event is the last at the Olympics until 2012 in London.

DAN THE HURDLE MAN

Dan Kinsey wins the 110-meter hurdles at the 1924 Paris Olympics. A St. Louisan and a former Big 10 champion while at the University of Illinois, Kinsey's greatest contributions may have been academic rather than athletic. He later becomes a college professor who pioneers the field of physical education.

NEVER SAY DYE

Continuing the city's strong tradition of producing 110-meter hurdle winners, Leighton Dye wins the national championship in 1926 and finishes fourth in the event at the 1928 Olympics despite briefly resetting the world-record best time. The University of Southern California alum is considered to be an important early hurdler who sets high standards for the US team.

STEPHENS AND BLAND

Helen Stephens becomes the "fastest woman in the world" at the 1936 Summer Olympics in Berlin. Born in Fulton, Missouri, the 18-year-old Stephens scorches to gold medals in the 100-meter dash and the 400-meter relay. Stephens later makes her home in St. Louis, where she passes away in 1994. The 1936 US Track and Field team also features St. Louisan Harriet Claiborne Bland, who competes in the 100-meter relay.

TROST MAKES THE MOST

CREDIT: AL TROST

Al Trost, a McCluer North High alum, plays with the US Men's National Soccer Team at the 1972 Munich Olympics. Trost scores twice in qualifying play and then earns a pair of Olympic caps. Trost played at SLU until 1970 and then held off on turning pro in order to play at the games. Pictured: Trost playing versus Pele when the Brazilian superstar visits as a member of the New York Cosmos and plays against the St. Louis Stars in the mid-1970s.

Boeckmann Among Men

The first female coach of the US Track and Field Team? A St. Louisan named Dee Boeckmann. Elected on a ballot that also featured men, she oversees male and female track and field athletes at the 1936 Olympics. An alum of Harris-Stowe State University and Washington University, Boeckmann coaches not only Stephens and Bland but also Jesse Owens, the African American sprinter whose skill and courage propel him to four gold medals at the Nazi-hosted Berlin games.

A BILL INTRODUCED IN THE SENATE

Crystal City's own Bill Bradley wins gold at the 1964 Olympic Games in Tokyo. A Princeton alum and future New York Knick, the six-foot, five-inch Bradley represents the United States in global sporting competition. He then goes on to represent the people of New Jersey as a senator from 1979 to 1997.

Bullet Bob and Ivory Crockett

Ivory Crockett is perhaps the greatest sprinter to never appear in an Olympics. Born in Tennessee but raised in Webster Groves, Crockett runs collegiately at Southern Illinois University–Carbondale, earning the Saluki program individual sprint titles. He runs a nine-second 100-yard dash in 1974, breaking the world record set by Bullet Bob Hayes at an AAU event in St. Louis in 1963. Crockett's record still stands.

JJK WASN'T JK

The Jackie Joyner-Kersee era of US Track and Field begins at the 1984 LA Games. JJK, an icon from East St. Louis, earns six medals, including three golds, across four Olympics in the next 12 years. She wins gold in the long jump in Seoul in 1988. She follows that by capturing gold in the heptathlon, an event she wins again in 1992. Her 7,291 points in the Seoul heptathlon remain a world record.

THE JACKIE JOYNER-KERSEE FOUNDATION

JJK's post-track career has been even more successful. Through the Jackie Joyner-Kersee Foundation, she has impacted countless lives in the St. Louis area. "The limitations of a city shrouded in stereotypes don't have to limit the course of a child's future," reads the mission statement of her foundation. "Their first steps to greatness start here."

Blades of Gloooria

Whether it's skating for fun at Steinberg Ice Rink or dreaming of becoming a pioneering ice dancer like St. Louisan Brandon Mroz, figure skating has found a toehold in St. Louis. The Savvis Center plays host to the US Figure Skating Championships, where skaters compete for spots on the Olympic team, in 2006. The St. Louis Sports Commission has announced that Enterprise Center will host the event again in 2026.

RAY ARMSTEAD

Ray Ricky Armstead is part of the 1984 Olympics 4 × 400 gold-medal team at the Los Angeles games. His four-man team runs a 2:57.91 to edge Great Britain and Nigeria. A Central Visual and Performing Arts high school alum, Armstead runs just one year of college track at Truman State before going on to Olympic glory. He has given back to the community by working as an art teacher in the Hazelwood school district.

Sweet Sauerbrunn

Lori Chalupny, Becky Sauerbrunn, and the USWNT take a second straight gold medal in London in 2012. Sauerbrunn, a Ladue alum who also played with J.B. Marine, is an played in college at the University of Virginia. She earns the gold plus two World Cups while anchoring the US defensive line in her stellar career. She serves as the USWNT captain in the early 2020s, and Ladue names its new soccer field "Becky Sauerbrunn Field" in 2022.

LORI LORE

Lori Chalupny wins a gold medal in Beijing at the 2008 Olympics. The Nerinx Hall alum, who plays club ball with J.B. Marine, stars at the University of North Carolina before joining the US Women's National Soccer Team. Chalupny steps up as a defender and even a scorer, netting a goal in the semifinal game en route to gold at the Beijing games. She later plays professionally for St. Louis Athletica.

CREDIT: DAVE ATKINSON VIA WIKIMEDIA COMMONS

COLLEEN QUIGLEY

A Nerinx Hall alum and a nine-time All-American at Florida State, Colleen Quigley has enjoyed a remarkable career. A National Indoor Championship winner in the mile in 2019, an Olympian in steeplechase in Rio, and part of an American 4 × 1500 squad that has shattered world records, Quigley has redefined expectations around distance running the world over.

Biles at the Trials

The 2021 US Olympic gymnastics girls prep for Tokyo at the Dome at America's Center in downtown St. Louis, where the team holds its final trials. The event features the greatest gymnast ever, Simone Biles, who later marries a St. Louisan—NFL safety Jonathan Owens.

THE OLYMPICS ARE FOR EVERYONE

CREDIT: SAINT LOUIS UNIVERSITY/SARAH CONROY

Sarah Adam (pictured) is among eight area athletes to head to the 2024 Paralympic Games in Paris. Adam and her squad capture a silver medal on the women's side. St. Louisan Eric Newby represents the US Men's Wheelchair Rugby team once again on the men's side, winning the third silver of his illustrious career.

RACING

Whether you're Richard Petty or Ricky Bobby, you want to go fast. Turns out, making tracks in a river city is easy to do. St. Louis has a rich auto racing history. The town was once a car manufacturing powerhouse. Local legends like Jerry Clinton and the Wallace family have helped the city's racing scene grow and flourish. From the speedway to the dirt track, motor sports in St. Louis are revving their engines stronger than ever.

FRIDAY NIGHT (HEAD)LIGHTS!

Walsh Stadium on Oakland Avenue comes alive with racing events on Friday nights in the 1930s. Walsh plays host to SLU football and a one-fifth mile track. The 1930s are also the decade that Jerry Clinton is born. Clinton is a successful driver on the professional Trans-Am Series and a major promoter for racing overall. A fixture on the St. Louis sports scene, the Washington University alum also has an Anheuser-Busch distributorship that makes him well known across the city.

Car Capital

St. Louis is America's car co-capital with Detroit in the middle of the 1900s. Nearly three quarters of a million cars come off St. Louis lines in the mid-1960s. The city is a pace car in the automotive world. Decades earlier, the city is the first in America with a gas station open to ordinary, everyday drivers.

WORLDWIDE, WORLD-CLASS

In 2019, the facility originally known as International Raceway is reopened as World Wide Technology Raceway. The facility sets a standard for the rest of the country in racing. As the raceway's website states, they are "just 5 minutes from Downtown St. Louis." WWT Raceway provides awesome access to world-class racing for St. Louis fans.

INTERNATIONAL EVEL

International Raceway is completed in 1967. Initially a drag strip, the raceway evolves into a quarter-mile speedway that hosts NASCAR, IndyCar, drag racing, and even stunt events. Evel Knievel baptizes the track. He jumps 10 cars on a Harley-Davidson motorcycle two days in a row in the summer of 1972.

CREDIT: ISC IMAGES & ARCHIVES VIA GETTY IMAGES

NEVER GOT RUSTY

Rusty Wallace is the greatest individual NASCAR racer ever to come out of St. Louis. He wins 55 races over his 20-plus-year career and leads more laps than all but six NASCAR drivers ever. He races his Gatorade car to a 1984 Rookie of the Year award and then drives it for over 20 years to the NASCAR Hall of Fame.

CREDIT: TED VAN PELT VIA WIKIMEDIA COMMONS

Family Wallace

The Wallaces are icons in the world of auto racing. Tracing their roots to Arnold and Fenton, they are known and celebrated across the world. Russ Wallace set a standard in short-track pro racing that is almost impossible to match. His children and grandchildren are legendary. Rusty is a former NASCAR Rookie of the Year and the 1989 Winston Cup champ. Kenny is a 25-year vet of NASCAR racing and a popular commentator. Mike races nearly 20 years on the NASCAR Cup series and 27 years on the NASCAR Xfinity series. Matt, Chrissy, and Steve Wallace have stamped their legacies on racing history as well.

MAMA

And let's not forget about mom! Russ's wife, Judy, pictured here with her ridiculously fast family, has created a racing dynasty unmatched in America.

CREDIT: DEREK BURGESS

KENNY

In 1991, Kenny Wallace wins the Spring 200. It is the first of nine wins for him in the next 10 years on the NASCAR Xfinity Series. He has worked with Fox and MRN Radio as a commentator for numerous racing events. His national broadcasting platform has made him one of the most recognized names in the sport.

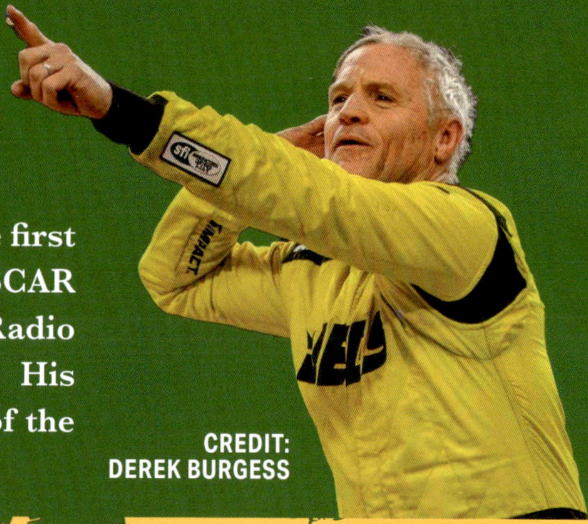

CREDIT: DEREK BURGESS

BOMMARITO AUTOMOTIVE GROUP 500

Scott Dixon wins the Bommarito Automotive Group 500 in 2023. Dixon's record-breaking performance comes in front of 100,000 people who turn out for the race in person and 25 times that many who tune in on TV.

DIRT TRACK HALL OF FAME

CREDIT: ST. LOUIS DIRT TRACK RACING HALL OF FAME

Established in 2023, the St. Louis Dirt Track Racing Hall of Fame celebrates dirt track racing in the area. As founder Derek Burgess says, "St. Louis has a a large racing history that a lot of people don't know about. . . . There are six dirt tracks within about an hour of the Arch that race on a weekly basis." Among the first inductees is Russ Wallace. His record-breaking performances at Tri-City Speedway may never be matched.

NASCAR CUP

The Enjoy Illinois 300 at WWT Raceway brings in Richard Petty to cut the opening ribbon in 2022. Joey Logano runs away with a rubber-burning victory as WWT plays host to the NASCAR Cup Series. The prestigious event announces to the world that St. Louis will continue to be a major player in auto racing.

Gettin' Dirty

The Dome at America's Center hosts the 2024 Gateway Dirt Nationals, an event it will host again in December of 2025. The three-day championship has become embedded in the hearts of dirt track fans, the most passionate of whom simply refer to it as "Dirt in December."

CREDIT: DEREK BURGESS

SWIMMING

Whether the water has been smooth or choppy, St. Louis's swimming history is rich, as you might expect from a river town. Take a dip or go for a plunge . . . you'll find over-the-top characters and some of the most serious competitors in the world. From Marquard Schwarz to Tom Jager and beyond, St. Louis swimming continues to freestyle its way across Olympic lengths and dive deeper than ever before.

NATATORIUM

The old St. Louis Natatorium on 19th and Chestnut gives St. Louisans a chance to swim in the 1880s. The Natatorium boasts a 40-by-140-foot pool. This early version of a St. Louis swimming facility reminds us that our swimming history runs a lot deeper than just 11 feet.

SWIMMERS YEAR

The 1904 Summer Olympics feature 10 medal events. Local swimmer Marquard Schwarz earns a bronze as part of an American relay team. The USA's Charles Daniels wins gold in the 220- and 440-yard freestyle events. Emile Rausch racks up four golds competing under the German empire's flag. He finishes with the most gold medals of any swimmer.

Don't Drink the Water

Multiple swimmers report getting seriously ill after swimming in the lake at Forest Park. At that point, the lake is still a dumping point for agricultural waste. The World's Fair also features gondola rides, giving the crowd a chance to swim accidentally.

TAKE THE PLUNGE

The 1904 Olympics are the first to feature diving and the last to feature "plunging." The American Swimming Association describes the key to plunging as "glid[ing] face downward for a period of 60 seconds without imparting any propulsion to the body from the arms and legs."

EASIER TO PLAY WITHOUT HORSES

Did you know that St. Louis was the first US city to host a water polo event? The noble sport features horses demonstrating their swimming skills . . . no, wait; that's a different kind of polo. And a wet one. In the real deal, teams compete in the lake at Forest Park at the 1904 Olympics. The Missouri Athletic Club takes the bronze. The MAC later hosts water polo championships itself in the 1920s, the first of their kind in America.

MAKOS SWIM TEAM

Today the Makos swim team provides a place for African American swimmers. Their recreational swim team begins in 2014, and it has since grown into a year-round swim team. The team practices at the O'Fallon Park and Rec Complex YMCA (four days a week) and Bayer YMCA (one day a week).

CREDIT: SLUH ATHLETICS

CALL ME MARCO THE WAY I OWN POLO

Today, water polo is a great high school sport. SLUH has dominated the prep water polo scene, winning 22 state titles. In recent years, the team has battled tooth and nail with the Parkway school district, which is no stranger to the water. Parkway West girls win six straight state titles in the 1970s and '80s in swimming, and Parkway West boys win four straight in the '80s.

Rams in Water

In the 1950s and '60s, Ladue High wins seven straight state swimming titles. Not coincidentally, Jim Halliburton is born, perhaps in water, in 1959. Halliburton goes undefeated while at Ladue High School and is a four-time All-American at Indiana University. He becomes the longest-tenured coach in SLU history and later coaches at Washington University. Halliburton remains perhaps the greatest swimmer in St. Louis history.

CREDIT: LADUE SCHOOL DISTRICT COMMUNICATION DEPARTMENT

CREDIT: MAKOS SWIM TEAM

ST. LOUIS SWIMS ON

Makos competes all over the United States. The program became a YMCA/USA competitive team in the early 2020s, increasing opportunities for swimmers to receive swimming scholarships to college. The hope for the future is that it will provide everyone a chance. Through efforts like Makos, St. Louis is swimming toward that goal.

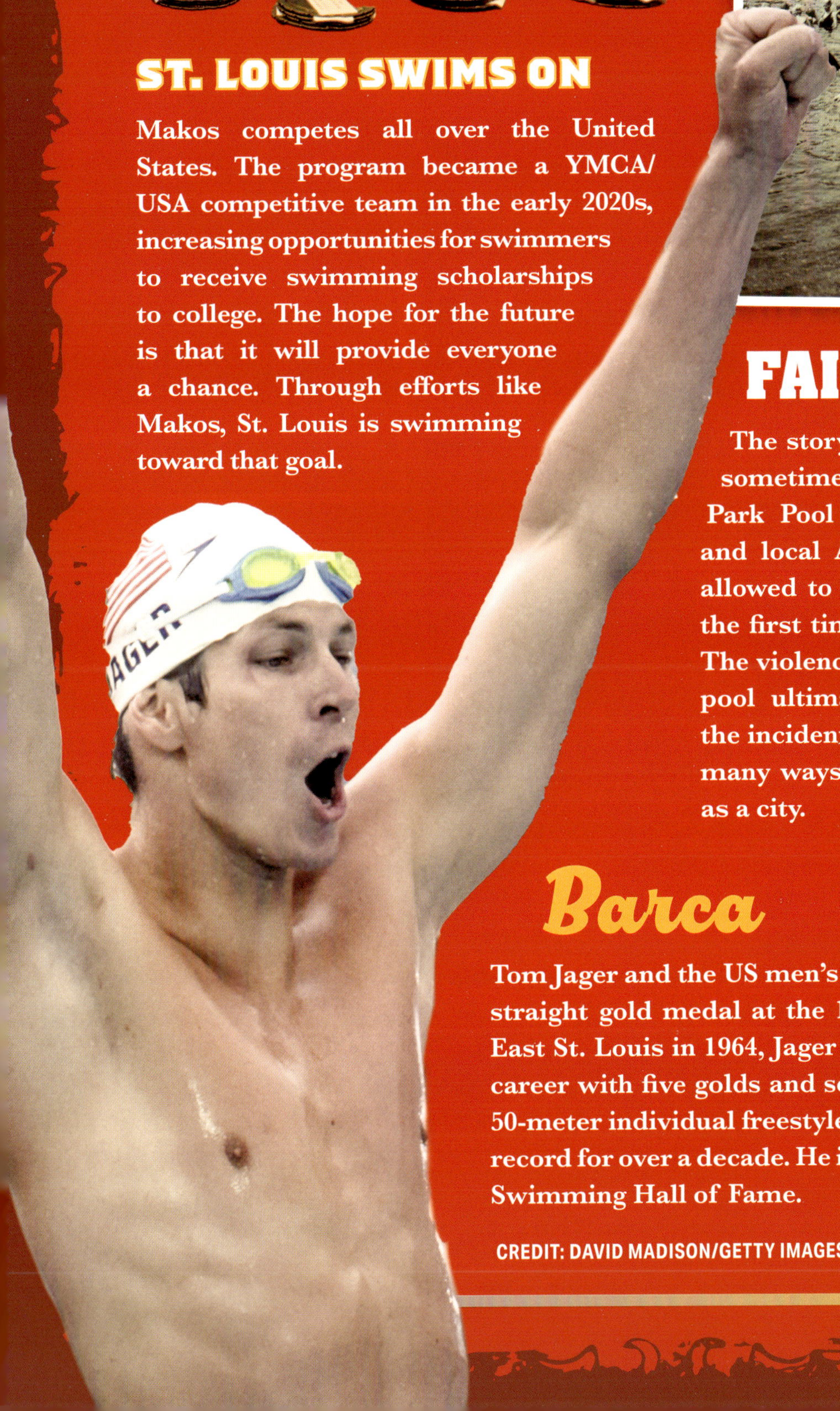

FAIRGROUND

The story of swimming in St. Louis has sometimes been unjust. The Fairground Park Pool is desegregated in the 1940s, and local African American children are allowed to swim at the historic venue for the first time. But a racist mob interferes. The violence is eventually stopped, but the pool ultimately closes down because of the incident. Fairground reminds us of the many ways in which we still have to grow as a city.

Barca

Tom Jager and the US men's 4 × 100 relay team earns a third straight gold medal at the 1992 Barcelona Games. Born in East St. Louis in 1964, Jager finishes his decorated Olympic career with five golds and seven medals overall. His record 50-meter individual freestyle time of 21.8 seconds is a world record for over a decade. He is a member of the International Swimming Hall of Fame.

CREDIT: DAVID MADISON/GETTY IMAGES

TENNIS

The history of tennis has a baseline called St. Louis. There are few other American cities that can claim the kind of heritage that St. Louis has. From the godfather of the Davis Cup, Dwight F. Davis, to champion and activist Arthur Ashe, St. Louis has given the world some of the game's biggest icons and most intriguing moments. Our city is a powerhouse of development in the mid-1900s, and the game continues to thrive here today. St. Louis is living, breathing proof that a tennis score and tennis lore both start with love.

DWIGHT DAVIS

St. Louisan Dwight F. Davis becomes the driving force behind the first Davis Cup. The Davis Cup is the biggest international men's team-tennis tournament in the world. The inaugural event in 1900 has grown to 155 teams in 2023. It is now a world championship event. The Davis Cup celebrates its 125th anniversary in 2025.

NEW TO THE FOREST

The first municipal tennis courts in the United States are opened in Forest Park in 1912. Davis is the man in charge of the project. An Olympian in 1904, Davis has a vision of a grand, inclusive future for his sport. The tennis courts in Forest Park are named after him.

Tennis at the Olympics

Beals C. Wright wins the gold medal at the 1904 Summer Olympics in St. Louis. Francis Field on the campus of Washington University hosts the action. Born in Boston, Wright finds a home in this area and passes away in Alton, Illinois.

A Champion of Grass and Concrete

Ted Drewes Sr. knows custard and tennis. The man who makes concretes delicious is also incredible on grass. Drewes dominates St. Louis tennis in the 1920s and 1930s. He wins the annual Muny Championships for 12 straight years from 1925 to 1936. He's also a four-time National Public Parks Singles Champion.

HART'S (RACKET) STRINGS

Doris Hart ascends to the world No. 1 ranking. Her accomplishments include 35 Grand Slam titles and 67 Grand Slam finals. Born in St. Louis in 1925, she sparkles in a Wimbledon doubles championship in 1947. Hart's career leads to induction in the International Tennis Hall of Fame in 1969.

Fire of Ashe

Arthur Ashe graduates as valedictorian from Sumner High School in 1961. The champion tennis player becomes the first man ever to win the men's singles title at the US Open. The Australian Open and Wimbledon follow, both firsts for an African American man. A member of the St. Louis Tennis Club, Ashe hones his skills and builds his competitive fire at the Armory. One of the best men's tennis players of all time, he is an 11-time participant in the Davis Cup and an inductee into the International Tennis Hall of Fame.

BRASH BASHER OF BELLEVILLE

Jimmy Connors is born in Belleville in 1952. He is the greatest men's tennis player ever to come from the St. Louis area. Connors enjoys a 25-year professional career and maintains his world No. 1 ranking for a record 160 weeks in the mid-1970s. He wins five US Opens. Originally coached by his mother, Gloria, Connors is the toughest tennis player who ever lived, a macho maestro with a swing that's as smooth as a whisper.

THE ARMORY

The Armory is one of the premier tennis facilities in the country in the time of Doris Hart and Arthur Ashe. Featuring ample court space, the Armory becomes a base and a springboard to tennis greatness. No other individual facility in Missouri—or perhaps the country—holds as many stories.

CREDIT: JUSTIN BARR

The Flach

Growing up in Kirkwood, Ken Flach plays his college tennis at SIU–Edwardsville, where he wins three national singles titles and a national doubles title with Robert Seguso. The pair dominates doubles professional tennis in the 1980s. They win Wimbledon and the US Open titles twice each. The Flach-Seguso duo ascends to the No. 1 ranking in the world in 1985. They stand atop the podium as the gold medal winners at the 1988 Seoul Olympics.

EISEL IDOL

Mary-Ann Eisel from Ladue wins mixed doubles at the US Open in 1968. A Ladue and Washington University alum, Eisel triumphs at the national tournament with her partner Peter Curtis. The two get married the next year. A former semifinalist at Wimbledon, Eisel is also a star golfer. She wins multiple St. Louis district championships on the links.

WHERE'D YOU GO TO HIGH SCHOOL?

In St. Louis, you are legally obligated to mention Nelly and your high school as much as humanly possible. Two of the most impressive tennis programs in the state are at St. Joseph's Academy and Chaminade. Beginning under the direction of Rosemary Wellington in the 1970s, St. Joe's captures 17 state titles from 1976 to 2022, including seven from 1994 to 2001. Chaminade wins five straight state championships from 1988 to 1992.

MORE THAN TENNIS

Ashe's influence extends far beyond the tennis court. He speaks out against South African apartheid and is known for his outspokenness and courage in support of the causes he believes in. He is diagnosed with HIV and dies of AIDS after a failed blood transfusion in the late 1980s. His courage and dignity remain as an example for others.

Faces of Aces

Through the Davis Cup, tennis becomes a team sport in the 1990s, and this idea is expanded via World Team Tennis, the brainchild of champion and trailblazer Billie Jean King. St. Louis's WTT franchise is the St. Louis Aces. The Aces feature players like Anna Kournikova and play their home matches at Forest Park. They win the WTT championship in 1996.

SOCCER

For kids in St. Louis, soccer is a rite of passage and a way of life. We hold onto memories made on soccer fields like a ball secured in Roman Burki's big mitts. Those steamy days at St. Louis Youth Soccer Association and those chilly nights at Fenton Soccer Park feed our souls. They give us that extra oomph on our next shot, that final bit of gas on our next run.

The 2023 arrival of Major League Soccer in St. Louis marks an important moment. The past, present, and future in the story of St. Louis soccer comes together with the birth of St. Louis CITY. Our soccer story never leaves us, and we can't wait for what's next. Soccer, like life, runs on in the 314.

FRONT FOOT

The first soccer game played in St. Louis is held at Sportsman's Park in 1882. Unbeknownst to the two teams, the Hurleys and the Hornets, the game will usher in a new era of sports in the city. The original contest is played within walking distance of the future site of CITYPARK, where St. Louis's Major League Soccer franchise will begin play 140 years later.

EVERYONE GETS A MEDAL

The Olympics feature just three teams in 1904. Two of the three teams are from the United States, and both of those teams come from St. Louis. Between Christian Brothers College and St. Rose Parish, though, neither can claim the gold medal. Galt F.C. of Canada takes first place after beating the two St. Louis squads by a combined score of 11–0.

Ben Millers

The St. Louis Soccer League is formed. The 30-plus-year history of the St. Louis Soccer League sets a standard for soccer across the country. The league gives rise to teams like the Ben Millers, who win the National Challenge Cup (later renamed the Open Cup) in 1920.

SBF

The Stix, Baer and Fuller Football Club wins back-to-back-to-back National Challenge Cups in the early 1930s. The local club draws its name and sponsorship from a St. Louis department store. It features the ultra-skilled Billy Gonsalves, who plays in the first two World Cups in 1930 and 1934 with the United States Men's National team.

C'MON, REF!

Let's face it. As St. Louis soccer fans, we know the referee is almost never right. But when he's one of our own, we certainly want him to be. Enter Prudencio Garcia, or, as most everyone called him, Pete. In 1950, the longtime Carondolet resident becomes the first US ref to officiate a World Cup. And we know that he got every call right.

THE GAME OF THEIR LIVES

The United States upsets England at the 1950 World Cup in Brazil. Five players from St. Louis take the field that day and score an improbable 1-0 upset win. Frank "Pee Wee" Wallace, Gino Pariani, Charlie Colombo, Harry Keough, and Frank Borghi etch their names in soccer history at Belo Horizante. The team also features St. Louisan Bob Annis. They are inducted into the Missouri Sports Hall of Fame in 2001. The game is the subject of the book *The Game of Their Lives* as well as a feature film.

Frank Borghi

Frank Borghi is the spectacular goalie of the 1950 US World Cup team. He is also a former professional baseball player in the Cardinals organization, a Bronze Star and Purple Heart Medalist in World War II, and a lifelong resident of the Hill. From baseball catcher to World Cup keeper, Borghi teams with Gino Pariani, Frank "Pee Wee" Wallace, Charlie Colombo, and Bob Annis on the local side St. Louis Simpkins-Ford. Their club wins the National Challenge Cup in 1948 and 1950.

STARS OF THE '70S

The St. Louis Stars shine bright in the North American Soccer League. Owned and operated by Bob Hermann, the Stars represent this city's soccer glory. Starting in 1967, local players like Pat McBride hold their own in a league that features international icons like Pele and Johann Cruyff. The Stars call Busch Stadium and Francis Field at Washington University home before folding following the 1977 season.

Bob Guelker

The Saint Louis University Billikens men's soccer team lays claim to its first NCAA championship in 1959. Coached by Bob Guelker, the Billikens add four more under Guelker from 1960 to 1965. Guelker is succeeded by Harry Keough, who also wins five national titles in the 1960s and 1970s.

HERMANN TROPHY

Presented annually, the Hermann Trophy is the most prestigious individual award in men's and women's college soccer. The Missouri Athletic Club begins awarding the Hermann Trophy in 1967. Saint Louis University players win the men's trophy for five straight years from 1969 to 1973, and, in 2024–25, the finalists include St. Louis CITY forward Emil Jaaskelainen, who scores 23 goals that year at Akron.

THE FATHER OF ST. LOUIS SOCCER

Pat McBride represents the best of St. Louis soccer. A star at St. Louis U. High and an All-American at SLU, McBride is a vital piece of the St. Louis Stars. He proves that the locally born stars can compete with the best across the world. His work as a coach with SIUE and with the St. Louis Steamers grows the game immensely in the area. McBride is inducted into the United States Soccer Hall of Fame in 1994.

CREDIT: MISSOURI HISTORICAL SOCIETY

CREDIT: SIUE ATHLETICS

BRONZE BOOT

The Southern Illinois University–Edwardsville Cougars men's team wins the NCAA Division II national championship under Bob Guelker in 1972. The team repeats the feat in 1979, also under Guelker and this time at the Division I level. The era is the pinnacle of the "Bronze Boot" rivalry between SIUE and SLU. In 1980, 22,512 spectators flock to Busch Stadium for the annual game, which relocates to CITYPARK in 2023.

CREDIT: FLORISSANT VALLEY COMMUNITY COLLEGE

CREDIT:
MISSOURI HISTORICAL SOCIETY

FLO VALLEY

Among all the college programs in the area, St. Louis Community College at Florissant Valley of the 1960s, 1970s, and 1980s may be the most impressive. The team is coached by Pete Sorber and wins five of six national championships between 1967 and 1972. The program wins 10 national championships by 1990. Flo Valley features players like Steve Pecher, who wins a state championship at Normandy and the national junior college championship at Flo Valley in 1975.

Set Sail

The St. Louis Steamers debut in the Major Indoor Soccer League in 1979. The team is originally owned by Marvin Mann, but ownership transfers to a group headed by Cardinals legend Stan Musial in 1980. The team becomes a staple in downtown St. Louis at the Checkerdome, with crowds 12,000+ coming out to see the Steamers play each night.

STEAMERS

The Steamers feature memorable players like Slobo Ilijevski, Don Ebert, Carl Rose, Ty Keough, Gary Edmonds, Jim Leishman, Kidd Fester, Sam Bick, Redmond Lane, Tony Bellinger, Jeff Cacciatore, Jim Tietjens, Don Droege, and Toni Glavin. They are coached by former St. Louis Star and soccer icon Al Trost, and they reach the league finals in three of their first four seasons under the Musial ownership group. The team remains a part of the St. Louis sports fabric until 1988.

CREDIT: DENVER POST VIA GETTY IMAGES

CREDIT: SUNSHINE LEMANEK

AMBUSH

Dr. Abraham Hawatmeh and Dr. Richard Rende relocate their pro indoor soccer team, and the St. Louis Ambush are formed in 1992. Stars like Daryl Doran, Jamie Swanner, Kevin Hundelt, and Mark Moser make the National Professional Soccer League their own. They win a championship in 1995 as part of a dominant decade. The brand and name are resurrected when the current St. Louis Ambush begin play at the St. Charles Family Arena in 2013.

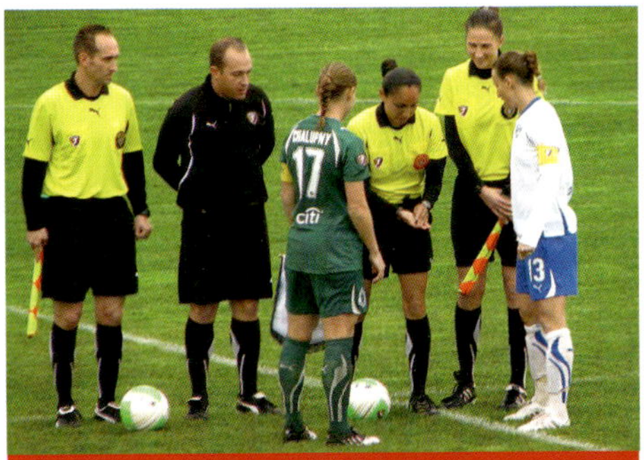

ATHLETICA

St. Louis Athletica begins play in Women's Professional Soccer, the top-flight American league that is launched in 2009. Athletica plays at Ralph Korte Stadium in Edwardsville and makes a more permanent home at Soccer Park in Fenton. The team's star is St. Louisan Lori Chalupny, who helps defend a goal occupied by US Women's National Team teammate Hope Solo.

Taylor Twellman

Taylor Twellman is a multisport star at Saint Louis University High in the 1990s. A future striker on the US Men's National Team, he actually goes to Maryland on a baseball scholarship. The son of NASL player Tim Twellman, Taylor is also a pretty good soccer player. In fact, he blooms into one of the finest strikers in the history of St. Louis soccer. A multi-time MLS Cup finalist, Twellman's professional career is cut short by concussion complications. He has dedicated his post-playing career to concussion research through his foundation ThinkTaylor. Twellman serves as a broadcaster for Apple TV's MLS coverage.

CREDIT: SLUH ATHLETICS

CREDIT: JUSTIN BARR

SLU WOMEN'S SOCCER

The Billikens go on a run for the ages from 2018 to 2024. The Billikens claim seven Atlantic 10 titles in a row in that span. Playing at Hermann Stadium, stars like Maddie Pokorny and Lyndsey Heckel lead the team on an unprecedented run of two-decade success.

STLFC

St. Louis Football Club begins play in the United Soccer League in 2015. STLFC is coached originally by Dale Schilly. The team draws solid fan interest, especially from the supporters group the St. Louligans, and plays at Soccer Park until 2020. STLFC is owned by Saint Louis University soccer alum Jim Kavanaugh. He becomes part of St. Louis CITY SC ownership later in the decade.

#MLS4THELOU

St. Louis CITY SC becomes the newest franchise in Major League Soccer in 2019. Led by Carolyn Kindle and the Taylor family, the ownership group launches big plans, including designs for CITYPARK. The 22,500-person venue in Downtown West is constructed over the next few years. The franchise is the first major professional sports organization in the United States with a majority-female ownership group.

CREDIT: ST. LOUIS CITY SC

CREDIT: ST. LOUIS CITY SC

NEXT

The expectations are high for St. Louis's first MLS-affiliated reserve team in 2022. The St. Louis CITY2 team is led by future CITY coach John Hackworth and players like captain Josh Yaro and winger Celio Pompeu. CITY2 races to an MLS NEXT Pro Western Conference postseason crown. Playing at Hermann Stadium and Ralph Korte Field, CITY2's excellence in MLS NEXTPro charts the course for future success.

GATES OF HELL AND BRAD CARNELL

Twelve of the CITY's 17 wins in the team's first season come at CITYPARK, which Lutz Pfannenstiel dubs "the Gateway to Hell" because of the raucous atmosphere. CITY's first manager, Bradley Carnell, and the team take the league by storm with upbeat energy, a high-press system, and unorthodox lineup mixing that keeps opponents on their back foot.

Carolyn Kindles the Fire

St. Louis has a long history of strong female ownership in sports. From Helene Britton to Georgia Frontiere, visionary women have made all the difference in St. Louis sports. Carolyn Kindle is the latest. Owner and CEO of St. Louis CITY, her tireless efforts in the late 2010s help bring #MLS4TheLou.

CREDIT: ST. LOUIS CITY SC

INAUGURAL SEASON

In 2023, St. Louis CITY opens MLS play by becoming the first team in league history to win its first five games. Featuring former Borussia Dortmund goalie Roman Burki, MLS mainstays like defender Tim Parker, and local products like midfielder Miggy Perez, CITY goes on to an amazing season. CITY is the first major-league expansion team in any sport to win its regular season conference title in its inaugural year.

IN LUTZ WE TRUST

CITY's first sporting director, Lutz Pfannenstiel, has enjoyed a long and colorful career that includes playing, managing, serving in front offices, and broadcasting soccer across the world. He is the only player to have appeared in FIFA-sanctioned leagues on six continents. His shrewd moves and roster tweaks inspire the often-repeated phrase "In Lutz We Trust" early in the club's history.

CREDIT: M. DONATO/FC BAYERN VIA GETTY IMAGES

CREDIT: ST. LOUIS CITY SC

Parker

MLS veterans are expected to decline once they hit 30. CITY center back Tim Parker defies those expectations in the inaugural CITY season. The journeyman Parker scores the first goal in CITY MLS history. He heads in a February corner kick against Austin and uses his goal celebration to announce that he and his wife are expecting a baby, who is born later in the season.

CREDIT: ST. LOUIS CITY SC

ROMAN EMPIRE

CITY's record-setting first season would not have been possible without the wizardry of Roman Burki. He lives up to his reputation after Pfannenstiel labels him "the best keeper in MLS history." He dazzles CITY supporters with athletic saves and incomparable distributions on the way to an MLS Goalkeeper of the Year award.

MIGGY

Teenage sensation Miguel Perez emerges as a local star for CITY in 2023. The youngster, whom sporting director Lutz Pfannenstiel discovered in a "cornfield" at an Olympic Development Program tournament, electrifies CITYPARK with a June goal to solidify a 3–1 win over the Vancouver Whitecaps. Having graduated from Pattonville High just weeks before the goal, Perez and his celebration earn the loudest cheer of the season from the capacity CITY crowd.

CREDIT: ST. LOUIS CITY SC

CREDIT: ST. LOUIS CITY SC

SUPPORTERS

Supporters fill CITYPARK, instantly creating the best atmosphere in Major League Soccer. Groups like the St. Louligans, St. Louis Punks, STL Santos, Fleur de Noise, No Nap City Ultras, and STL Thieves bring the noise, the passion, and the fun, marching into each home match to root on the City Boyz.

CREDIT: ST. LOUIS CITY SC

CITY LEEEADS

With the emergence of St. Louis CITY, soccer once again fills the airwaves on Y98 and on Apple TV. I forget the name of the loud guy who calls those games. The host of the pre- and post-game shows is Jennifer Siess and the color commentator and analyst is Dale Schilly. But what about the loud guy who says "CITY LEEEADS!"? I'll look his name up later.

CREDIT: ST. LOUIS CITY SC

CITY FUTURES

St. Louis CITY is committed to growing the game in the St. Louis metro area and beyond. The team's CITY Futures program "encompasses a number of community programs intended to promote soccer in the region, make soccer accessible to all in St. Louis, and help invest in the community through soccer." In addition, CITY has partnered with the US Soccer Federation to build mini pitches that encourage youngsters to get active and play the sport recreationally.

2024 and Beyond

The Washington University Women's Soccer Team clinches its second-ever national championship with a convincing 3–0 win over William Smith in December 2024. The victory represents the 26th national championship across all sports for the Bears and Lady Bears. More than that, the win signifies the enduring potential of youth soccer in St. Louis. The team is honored at a St. Louis CITY game to start 2025.

SOFTBALL

Softball is one of the the most popular recreational sports in St. Louis. Everybody and their mother belongs to a rec league softball team. But did you know that St. Louis was once home to an orange-clad professional softball team in the late 1970s? Whether it's the pro Hummers or Saint Louis University Billikens softball, this city is always ready to step into the box or the pitcher's circle.

CREDIT: MISSOURI HISTORICAL SOCIETY

BLUES SOFTBALL

St. Louis women's softball booms in World War II and afterward. The St. Louis Blues, together with their sponsor Kutis Funeral Homes, and charismatic players like the iconic and inimitable pitcher Betty Woods make the game even more popular in the late 1950s and early 1960s.

CREDIT: MISSOURI HISTORICAL SOCIETY

The Hummers

The St. Louis Hummers are one of the best stories out of 1970s St. Louis. Playing at Harrawood in Valley Park, the team competes in the International Women's Professional Softball Association (IWPSA) and does well. They make the playoffs in 1977, 1978, and 1979 and go to the championship series in '78 and '79.

HUMMING ALONG

Owned by Gayle Harrawood and coached by Bob Umfleet, the Hummers delight fans at Hummers Park, their 5,000-seat venue. Shortstop Debbie Zoss praises the team's togetherness and balance over the three years, saying other teams "have to watch out for everyone" on the squad. The roster is maintained by General Manager George W. Jones.

PATTY RAKES

Patty Guenzler is the star of the league, winning a batting title with a .398 mark in 1977. She does even better the next year, racking up a .404 average. It's not a short season, either. The Hummers are involved in 98 games in their second year of existence, playing teams like the Chicago Ravens and Michigan Travelers. The Hummers stamp a ticket to the IWPSA World Series by winning 55 games in 1978.

Linda Wells

A pitcher for the Hummers, Pacific native Linda Wells plays softball at Southeast Missouri State. Oh yeah, she plays volleyball, tennis, field hockey, and basketball as well. An incredible athlete, she pitches for the Hummers before going on to coach at Minnesota and Arizona State. With more than 900 NCAA coaching wins, she is one of the greatest college softball coaches ever.

CREDIT: BILL GREENBLATT/ST. LOUIS SPORTS HALL OF FAME

HUM ON

Teams like the Hummers have paved the way for girls and women in professional sports. Though the Hummers do not continue into the 1980s, their legacy lives on. St. Louis loves its softball, and, for a time, we have one of the very best teams in the nation.

KHOURY SOFTBALL

Like Linda Wells, many young St. Louisans have cut their teeth in Khoury Softball Leagues. Dating back to George Khoury's idea for baseball in the 1930s, the nonprofit creates its first softball leagues in the late 1950s. The Khoury Leagues' international headquarters remain on Lemay Ferry.

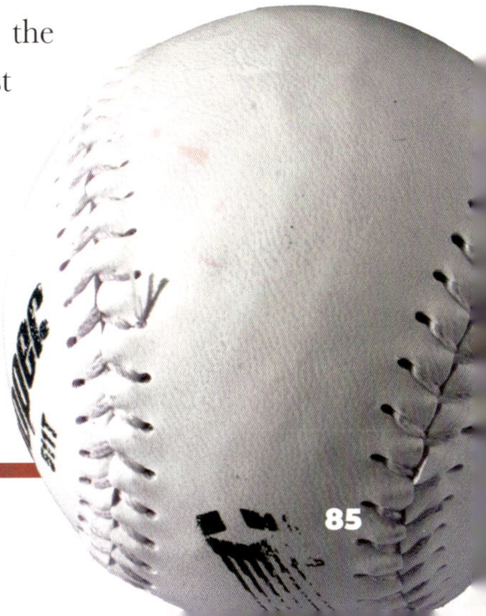

CREDIT: ROCKWOOD SCHOOL DISTRICT

LANCERS WITH BATS

The Lafayette Lancers softball program is the only St. Louis program to win back-to-back state titles twice. The program captures state titles in 1978 and 1979 before doing it again in 2000 and 2001. The Lancers win the 2024 state championship on a walkoff three-run home run by Riley Mulligan against Columbia Rock Bridge.

CREDIT: SAINT LOUIS UNIVERSITY SOFTBALL

DAWN

We're proud of being from the 314 . . . but are we as proud as Dawn Elser? Elser becomes the first-ever Saint Louis University Softball Hall of Famer, starring for the Billikens from 1986 to 1989. She is the only Billiken softball player to record a hit in 20 straight games. More impressively though, the girl from Belleville finishes her career with her university's area code as a batting average. By batting .405 her senior year, Elser hits exactly .314 in her time in a SLU jersey.

BURLY

Name me a pitcher who's won more than 700 games. There aren't that many. If you name Roy Burlison, of the St. Louis Browns fast-pitch softball team, then you're on to something. His mastery propels the Browns to a 1973 American Softball Association World Series berth. He stands as the best fast-pitch softball pitcher in Missouri history.

Connoyer

The longest-tenured head softball coach in Saint Louis University softball program history, Christy Connoyer has brought consistency and success to midtown. She guides the program to its first-ever Atlantic 10 title in 2023. That season, she earns the conference's Coach of the Year honor.

CREDIT: BILL BARRETT/SLU SOFTBALL

VOLLEYBALL

St. Louis volleyball has a strong tradition and fan base for both the men's and women's games. Incredible coaches like Teri Clemens and outstanding players like Benishe Roberts have made a home in St. Louis. Whether it's high school kids cheering wildly for their friends at the state championship or pickup games played on the sand courts of Forest Park, St. Louis knows how to meet at the net. We bump, we set, we spike, and when it's over, we can't wait to invite you back to do it again. After all, Mikasa is su casa...

CREDIT: BILL GREENBLATT/ ST. LOUIS SPORTS HALL OF FAME

SIMPLY THE BEST

The greatest volleyball dynasty of the 1980s, Incarnate Word wins five straight girls state championships from 1982 to 1986 in the 3A division. The Red Knights are guided by Truman State alum Teri Clemens and later Karen Piedimonte. The team inspires awe as well as fear during the greatest high school volleyball run of the decade. Clemens goes on to coach the college program that owns the next decade.

Lady Lancers

The Lafayette Lady Lancers are among the very elite. Many programs have won a state championship. Few programs have a three-peat. But back-to-back three-peats? A six-peat? The Lady Lancers accomplish the feat from 2011 to 2016. They miraculously complete another three-peat in 2024.

CREDIT: TERRY SIMPSON

JR. BILLS

Missouri boys first play for a state championship in 1987. Kirkwood is the first champion. Saint Louis University High and Vianney rise in the 1990s and early 2000s as Class 4 volleyball powerhouses, winning a combined 11 state titles from 1997 to 2011. SLUH rattles off 76 straight wins beginning in 2019 and makes it five straight state championships in 2023.

Short Quest

The St. Louis Quest debut in 2002 as part of United States Professional Volleyball. With a home at Washington University Field House, they go 10–8 in their lone season. A second season is planned but fails to get off the ground at the Family Arena. League MVP Benishe Roberts is excellent in the team's 18 matches.

Teri Strikes Again

Washington University Women's Volleyball is the dominant Division III college program of the 1990s. From 1989 to 1996, the squad wins the national championship seven of eight years, including six straight times from 1991 to 1996. Led by Teri Clemens, the program hits absurd heights in a sustained run of success. The Lady Bears make 18 Final Four appearances from 1989 to 2016, winning 10 total national championships in that span.

THE TROJAN

Murphy Troy enjoys a successful volleyball career at Saint Louis University High and at the University of Southern California. He goes on to win gold with Team USA at the 2014 World League Championships in Florence and the 2015 Volleyball World Cup in Japan. He is also a member of the bronze-medal Olympic team in Rio De Janeiro.

TOUZINSKY

Scott Touzinsky competes from 2007 to 2012 as a member of the USA men's volleyball team. A Vianney alum, he goes on to become an ACE expert at Long Beach State, where he leads the team to a national championship final in his senior year. His career is one that demonstrates tenacity, longevity, and competitive fire. After overcoming a serious knee injury in his early 20s, he earns a gold medal at the 2008 Beijing Olympics with Team USA.

CREDIT: SCOTT TOUZINSKY

FOLKLORE

Kristin Folkl very well may be the best female athlete to ever come out of St. Louis. A St. Joseph's Angel, Folkl wins eight state championships between volleyball and basketball during her high school days. She is a volleyball All-American four times at Stanford and wins three national championships in that sport. In basketball, she makes another two Final Four trips and is an All-American as a senior. She is a two-sport academic All-American and goes on to play in the WNBA.

CREDIT: BILL GREENBLATT/ST. LOUIS SPORTS HALL OF FAME

Stallions

The St. Louis Stallions are a professional volleyball team competing in the Volleyball League of America. The Stallions are the area's first professional men's volleyball team. The franchise has major plans for growth in both the men's and women's games. The Stallions play their matches at the Beal Center in Chesterfield.

STALLIONS

BARTSCH-HACKLEY

Collinsville High alum Michelle Bartsch-Hackley wins gold at the Tokyo Olympics in 2021. Hackley stars at the University of Illinois before earning a spot on the national team. After failing to make the Olympic roster in 2016, the outside hitter perseveres to become part of the 2021 USA squad. That team outduels Italy in a gold-medal classic. She coaches at Ohio State while playing professionally with the Columbus Fury.

CREDIT: CRAIG PRESSMAN

WRESTLING

Pro wrestling is one of the most entertaining aspects of St. Louis sports. Like so much, it traces its roots back to the 1904 Olympics. By mid-century, St. Louis has the leading wrestling TV show in the world. From Sam Muchnick to Randy Orton, our characters, our rings, and our sense of fun have wrestled any doubt about our wrestling greatness down to the canvas.

Olympic Wrestlers

At the 1904 Olympics, 44 wrestlers compete for the wrestling gold medals. In the heavyweight division, Norwegian Bernhoff Hansen takes it. The X-Man, Frank X. Kugler, wins silver. Thirty-eight of the 44 wrestlers who compete at the games are American.

THESZ

A three-time National Wrestling Association (NWA) national champion and a six-time heavyweight champion, Aloysius Martin Thesz is born in Michigan in 1916. His family moves to St. Louis when he's a kid. Thesz hits the greatest heights that wrestling has to offer. He tours Japan, and audiences call him the "God of Wrestling." From National Gym in St. Louis to the heavens above Mount Fuji, Lou from the Lou is the best of his era.

MUCHNICK

As a boy, Sam Muchnick emigrates from Ukraine to St. Louis. In his 20s, he works as a reporter covering the Cardinals before transitioning to promotions. He serves two separate terms as president of the National Wrestling Alliance. He builds incredible enthusiasm for wrestling in Missouri. Pictured: a match in the 1930s just down the road in Sikeston.

Wrestling at the Chase

Wrestling at the Chase debuts on KPLR and becomes a massive television sensation. KPLR is the first network to broadcast live pro wrestling regularly. The show runs for close to 25 years. It shows off professional wrestling from the historic Chase Park Plaza hotel in the Central West End. Wrestling entertainers like Ric Flair and Dick the Bruiser help the show run until 1983.

CREDIT: JUSTIN BARR

St. Louis Wrestling Club

The St. Louis Wrestling Club is founded in 1959 and lasts until 1985. It is Sam Muchnick's creation. Harley Race is a minority owner, and the organization is boosted by St. Louisan Larry Matysik. His announcing, promoting, and marketing of the sport he loves make all the difference in the world to fans.

COWBOY BOB ORTON

Bob Orton and his brother Barry light up the NWA in the early 1980s. Cowboy Bob is one of the most colorful performers at the Chase. He is inducted into the WWE Hall of Fame in 2005, and his son Randy becomes one of the most popular wrestlers in the universe.

RIC FLAIR

Nature Boy. WOOOOOOOOOOOOOOO! Ric Flair is one of the most iconic wrestlers in American history. The worldwide phenomenon of Flair may not have been possible without St. Louis. He is the 1983 NWA Missouri Heavyweight champion, and many of his most famous moments, tricks, laughs, tears, triumphs, and stumbles trace back to this area. He is a 2007 inductee to the St. Louis Wrestling Hall of Fame.

STILL CHASING

In 2023, the Chase Park Plaza Hotel hosts the NWA 75th Anniversary Show. EC3 defeats Tyrus in a spectacular heavyweight title match. Whether at the Chase or the South Broadway Athletic Club, wrestling is still very much alive in St. Louis.

DICK THE BRUISER

One of the greatest names in professional sports history, Dick the Bruiser does more than just bruise people. A former Green Bay Packer, he dominates the professional wrestling scene in the 1950s, '60s, and '70s. Even his late-career matches, like a 1979 bout against Mike Bowyer at the Chase, are the talk of the circuit.

Vince McMahon

The World Wrestling Federation (WWF) comes to St. Louis and begins taping its highly rated TV programs at the Chase and Kiel Auditorium in the 1980s. It's the end of an era and the start of something new. Each twilight leads to a new dawn. WWF becomes WWE and grows into the wrestling mammoth that we know, love, and hate today.

Wrestling Hall of Fame

Under the guidance of Larry Matysik, the St. Louis Wrestling Hall of Fame launches in 2007at the South County Mall. It relocates the next year to the South Broadway Athletic Club. The initial class includes Muchnick and Flair, and the Class of 2024 includes such luminaries as ring announcer George Abel and two-time WWF champion Wendi Richter.

CREDIT: STL WRESTLING HALL OF FAME

2021 NCAA WRESTLING CHAMPIONSHIPS

Let's take a break from the fake stuff (uh, I mean the sort of real stuff that we all call real even though it's scripted. Don't sue me, Vince McMahon). Let's get to the actual, real wrestling. The Enterprise Center hosts the NCAA Wrestling Championships in 2021. The Iowa Hawkeyes win the championship in the 63-team field.

RANDY

St. Louisan Randy Orton is on top of the WWE in the 2010s. Part of Missouri's storied Orton wrestling family, Randy has a unique rivalry with John Cena. He becomes the youngest wrestler to win a heavyweight world title in 2014. An alum of Hazelwood Central, Orton remains an extremely popular name in WWE. He continues to make his home in St. Charles.

CREDIT: ETHAN MILLER/GETTY IMAGES

HONORABLE MENTIONS

If only they let me write a thousand pages. . . . I have filled documents with tremendous stories from St. Louisans of all backgrounds. As we head toward the finish line, there are some St. Louis sports that I have to note. Call them honorable mentions if you will. These are the sports that might not be top of mind for everyone, but for many they are top of heart.

BOCCE BALL

CREDIT: ITALIA AMERICA BOCCE CLUB

The Italia America Bocce Ball Club is an institution in its own right. Located on the Hill, it is bocce's heart in St. Louis. Bocce is a game that dates back several centuries before the time of Christ. The Italia America Bocce Ball Club hosts the sport's world championships in June 2018. And by the way, it's bocce as in "oh-chee." If you call it botch-ee, you botched it.

CREDIT: DAREL SHELTON

CORNHOLE

It's cornhole, OK? It isn't bags or anything else. Even though you throw bags. You throw them into the hole. Like corn! There is a thriving cornhole scene around St. Louis, from the pro game to every grillout you go to in May and June. St. Louis's game!

Curling

The St. Louis Curling Club calls Creve Coeur Ice Arena home. It has been helping to "build a culture and a community around curling" since the late 2000s. They offer beginners clinics as well as leagues like the Rogers Cup and the Friday Pizza League for curlers of all ages.

Cycling

Since the St. Louis Cycling Club was founded in 1887, the sport has been important to the city. Whether it's 1936–37 Missouri state champ Raymond Florman Jr. or 1960 Olympian Joe Becker, the city's rich tradition of producing, racing, and improving bicycles speeds on and on. Today, clubs like KewlBeanz Cycling (pictured) carry on a rich tradition of cycling for sport, friendship, and fun.

CREDIT: JOHN HACKWORTH

CREDIT: THE ST. LOUIS BOMBERS RUGBY CLUB

RUGBY

The St. Louis Bombers are the preeminent rugby club in St. Louis. In 2024, they capture the USA Rugby National Championship at the Division I level. Other area programs include the St. Louis Hornets, the St. Louis Crusaders, and, on the women's side, the St. Louis Sabres. Saint Louis University has featured rugby as a club sport since 1957.

GAELIC SPORTS

Founded in 2003, the St. Louis Gaelic Athletic Club "develops Irish sports and preserves Irish cultural heritage." Sports played by the club include the Irish national sport, hurling; hurling's sister sport, camogie; and the most popular Irish sport, Gaelic football.

CREDIT: ST. LOUIS GAELIC ATHLETIC CLUB

WASHERS

See St. Louis barbecues. Everybody's uncle's birthday party. It's a St. Louis game. You aim to get a score of 21 tossing the washers inside a cup (that's inside a box!) from at least several feet away. We know washers well in the 314. We know "warshers" too.

HORSESHOES

If you're out in Wentzville, check out the National Horseshoe Pitchers Association Hall of Fame. They enshrine the best of the best: Only two-time world champions have a chance to gain induction into the Hall.

JUDO

St. Louis Community College at Forest Park dominates the judo scene in the 1970s. The program wins the National Junior College Athletic Association championship in the sport five years running from 1972 to 1976. Judo is "the gentle way . . . an exciting and dynamic martial art that requires both physical strength and mental discipline," according to USA Judo.

Juggling

Thom Wall holds numerous records in the sport of juggling, including the longest sustained juggling of six knives. (Reference: I tried to juggle four knives and ended up having to fill oven mitts with Neosporin). A star juggler with Cirque Du Soleil and the Royal Caribbean cruise line, Wall moves to St. Louis with his family as a kid and graduates from Ladue Horton Watkins.

PICKLEBALL

Pickleball has entered full bloom in the United States, and St. Louis is central to the sport's expansion. The sport offers the young and old alike a slow pace with unlimited fun (and a fast track to ligament repair). The Dwight Davis Tennis Center in Forest Park now features four pickleball courts.

CREDIT:
THOM WALL_AVI PRYNTZ-NADWORNY

Index

KHOURY LEAGUE PROCLAMATION AT CITY HALL IN KIRKWOOD, MISSOURI

CREDIT: THE STATE HISTORICAL SOCIETY OF MISSOURI